D1569910

Career Launcher

Real Estate

Career Launcher series

Advertising and Public Relations
Computers and Programming
Education
Energy
Fashion
Film
Finance
Food Services
Hospitality
Internet
Health Care Management
Health Care Providers
Law
Law Enforcement and Public Safety
Manufacturing
Nonprofit Organizations
Performing Arts
Professional Sports Organizations
Real Estate
Recording Industry
Television
Video Games

Career Launcher

Real Estate

Natalie Davis and Kelly Kagamas Tomkies

Ferguson Publishing
An imprint of Infobase Publishing

Career Launcher: **Real Estate**

Ferguson
An imprint of Infobase Publishing
132 West 31st Street
New York NY 10001

331.7333
D263r

Library of Congress Cataloging-in-Publication Data

Davis, Natalie.
    Real estate / by Natalie Davis and Kelly Kagamas Tomkies. — 1st ed.
       p. cm. — (Career launcher series)
    Includes bibliographical references and index.
    ISBN-13: 978-0-8160-7966-7 (hardcover : alk. paper)
    ISBN-10: 0-8160-7966-8 (hardcover : alk. paper)
1. Real estate business—Vocational guidance. I. Tomkies, Kelly Kagamas.
II. Title.
    HD1375.D328 2010
    333.3023—dc22

                                          2010030524

Ferguson books are available at special discounts when purchased in bulk quantities for businesses, associations, institutions, or sales promotions. Please call our Special Sales Department in New York at (212) 967-8800 or (800) 322-8755.

You can find Ferguson on the World Wide Web at http://www.fergpubco.com

Produced by Print Matters, Inc.
Text design by A Good Thing, Inc.
Cover design by Takeshi Takahashi
Cover printed by Yurchak Printing, Landisville, Penn.
Book printed and bound by Yurchak Printing, Landisville, Penn.
Date printed: April 2011

Printed in the United States of America

10 9 8 7 6 5 4 3 2 1

This book is printed on acid-free paper.

Contents

Foreword

This is an interesting time for those starting a new career in real estate. We have all heard the news about falling markets. In one way or another we have all seen or experienced the troubles the 2008 and 2009 recession has caused. If you are serious about working in real estate, people around you may have tried to advise you against it. I am telling you: If you have the qualities needed to do well in this industry—along with a realistic view—recession or no, you can have a rewarding career. In many ways, this is the best time to learn real estate!

Let us start with reality. If you are reading this, you have probably heard all about the benefits of working in real estate—flexible hours, big commissions, being your own boss. You may even have heard stories about people becoming real estate millionaires. I will not say those days are over, but the market is shifting. If you can adapt to changing market conditions and respond appropriately, you will be further ahead of those with much more experience.

Right now, the market is one of short sales and foreclosures. Short sales involve a home selling for less than the amount the seller borrowed to buy the property, and with bank-owned properties known as foreclosures, the combination will make up 60 percent of the potential sales out there. Those looking for the easy sales and traditional methods of the past will be disappointed. We are not in a traditional market. It is in repair mode after the market booms of 2003 and 2004. Many believe those years were a real estate anomaly wherein home values rose 23 percent a year. No market can sustain that. If you look at the average in my area, Baltimore County, Maryland, the average appreciation of home value is nearly 4 percent. Some areas are different, but the average over the past 25 years is 4 or 5 percent per year. Presently, Baltimore-area home prices are at the 2004 level. If someone bought a house in 2000 and did not refinance or cash out and borrow finance in advance, they are fine. That homeowner is not losing money. Their home values in 2009 are still significantly better than they were in 2000. The point is there are good days ahead, for homeowners and for professionals in the field.

We are about to get the next wave of short sales and foreclosures. Three-year adjustable-rate mortgages are about to come through and now houses are not worth what they were. Some homeowners are in trouble—if they cannot refinance and cannot afford to stay in their house, they have little choice but to go the short-sale route.

It is important to remember that real estate is a long-term investment. Even people in the stock market will tell you that real estate remains a solid investment. Those in the market to buy are finding really good prices, and they are going to get better. You can find oceanfront property at one-third of what it would have been. A look at the entire inventory of available properties—condos, new constructions, and others—shows anything available is active on the market. At the current absorption rate, it will take 290 months to deplete the current inventory. Demand affects that, of course; but nationwide, for the first time in three years, we saw increased sales in May 2009. Things are getting better. Prices are stable and activity is up. In the Baltimore region, properties are selling fast in the $250,000 to $300,000 range—especially houses in model-like condition. First impressions are still important: even in a recession, "shiny pennies" are the ones people want to buy. That means there is still tremendous opportunity and value to be found.

I mention all of this to give you a clear look at where our industry is, at this time. As a pro in this field, you are dealing with the most important financial decision anyone will ever make. If, after reading this guide, you decide that you do want to make the move, great! We need good, solid people in our field, men and women who are hard-working, highly motivated, ethical, and honest. Even the best entrants will need a good support system, multi-faceted training, and thorough education. Now, I am totally biased about our business model at Keller Williams, where we focus on education and training and business models to follow. We teach regardless of a person's prior education. Although we may not coddle our associates, we do give them tremendous training. In real-estate terms, someone with less than four years in the field is considered a rookie.

There are financial realities as well for people entering the real-estate industry. There are certain investments you have to make—generally, expect that it will cost $6,000 to $10,000 for someone to get into this business. On top of that, you will have to deal with the reality that no one wants to be the brain surgeon's first patient. However, a qualified intern is much easier to work with than a medical student. Being a real estate novice is only a problem with folks if you appear to be unprepared or unqualified. If you are prepared and well-trained, you should thrive. Still, you must be realistic: you will need the ability to understand the importance of the absorption rate, the time it takes for inventory to be sold, and how to analyze the market.

With the Internet, homebuyers can do much of the information search for themselves. That means it is up to the real estate professional to show buyers what that information really means. Ultimately, it is about picking your properties through comparative market analysis. I tell people it is a market trend report—properties in certain markets trend differently in summer than they do in the spring. That is just logic. Cabin fever syndrome is a huge factor in winter. If January temperatures exceed 50 degrees three days in a row, our business is slammed. If January is cold and snowy, we will not get busy until the end of February. Fourteen years of experience show it.

If you are serious about pursuing real estate, explore your reasons why. Do you want to be the next Trump? (Good luck.) Are you looking to make a million dollars and not work hard? (Try something else.) Do you think your winning personality will be your ticket to success? (It will help, but you need more than that.) Your motivations need to be explored carefully before you leap. We have had people in this business for 25 to 30 years who have come to hate it because real estate is so high-tech now. People who need answers in 10 to 15 minutes are not patient with those who check messages at the end of the day. This, in many ways, is a "react" business. You have to, at the very least, appear to be available frequently and let technology help you give prospects the appearance that you can handle their questions 24/7. Make sure your expectations are realistic. Then, you will need to put together a business plan and be accountable to that plan.

The primary challenge is that, essentially, we are all subcontractors—we may work with a brokerage, but at the end we have to depend on ourselves and what we make is related to what we put into it. I think that going into real estate as a profession is much like the feeling of turning 18. We cannot wait for the chance to be accountable only to ourselves and not have someone else telling us what to do. Being self-employed, we only need to look in the mirror every day to evaluate how the employee is doing. Now, would we fire us based on the performance of the day? Having accountability makes sure you do what you say you are going to do.

This book will introduce you to many of the careers available under the real-estate category. There are many of them, but the primary function of the field is to generate business and sell property.

As a broker or agent, you are a salesperson. You need to accept that and be proud of it. Own it! Yes, moving a customer to settlement is part of the job, but generating leads—finding new prospects—is the most important activity. Some realty offices offer good systems for this; we certainly do at Keller Williams, where we create a "First 100 Days" plan with our new agents. We help them keep their goals and expectations in mind and prioritize information. They must earn a real estate license—our goal is to help them pass the test. Then, they must learn to do business—to be ready to go from a weekly paycheck to a 100 percent commission base. Many people start part-time because they cannot let go of the paycheck. That is why I recommend that you start with $6,000 to $10,000 in the bank. If you have six months of expenses in the bank and have a business plan you are committed to following and being accountable to, you will be okay.

Remember that being realistic is the key to avoiding failure. Being successful comes down to maintaining your checks and balances, doing what you say you will do, and staying committed to your plan. Winning is all about activity, learning something new every day, and being diligent in your efforts to get the job done. If you can do that, you can succeed in real estate. I wish you all good luck!

—Bob Kimball, Manager, Keller Williams Realty
PRESIDENT, GREATER BALTIMORE BOARD OF REALTORS

Acknowledgments

My deepest thanks go to Richard Rothschild of Print Matters, who treated this writer with care, respect, and compassion. I also send gratitude to my family and friends, Don Rauf, Bob Kimball, and all the people who generously shared their time, insights, experience, and good humor with me during this process. It would be remiss of me to omit the many people looking to make better lives for themselves and their families. You were in my mind every step of the way during the creation of this book, and I pray it provides the information you need to help you make your dreams reality.

—NATALIE DAVIS

Sincere thanks to Richard Rothschild for this opportunity, Michael Centore for his input and assistance, and my husband and family for their support.

—KELLY KAGAMAS TOMKIES

Introduction

So, you are considering a career in real estate. You are not alone: many Americans just like you contemplate making their mark in a real estate career. Young business school graduates see the potential for investment success and of becoming the next Donald Trump. Homemakers see the field as a way to earn income for their families while fulfilling their parenting responsibilities. Many retirees enter the industry to supplement fixed incomes. It makes sense that real estate would be a popular career choice. Think about it: When you meet successful individuals from the field, they tend to be enthusiastic about what they do. They appear prosperous. They look like they are having a good time at work. Agents and brokers are happy to talk about their successes, their commissions, some merrily boasting about the flexibility of their work schedules.

It all sounds like an ideal gig. There is more, though. Much of real estate's allure comes from the fact that it deals with more than selling land or houses. Real estate workers help people to attain their dreams—a happy, secure life for themselves and their families, and the sense of accomplishment that comes from owning property. Administrative staffers, researchers, counselors, and appraisers may not get the commission checks the top-producing brokers and agents do, but they know the satisfaction of helping people with one of the most significant investments of their lives. Real estate advertising and public relations professionals, often quite well paid, get to put their creative talents to good use. Industry pros can choose the environment in which they operate. Many work from their own homes, while others opt for small or large offices or as a part of a realty team. Additionally, real estate is a highly social field, not only in terms of dealing with homebuyers, but also in terms of networking with colleagues. For people persons, real estate can be a fun and rewarding occupation.

Although real estate is a field that admittedly has its ups and downs, it can never die. More than 2.5 million people in the United States currently make their living in real estate, according to a February 2009 U.S. Bureau of Labor Statistics report. That figure does not include ancillary positions such as administrative assistants and part-time workers, so one can assume that many more people are making a living performing those necessary functions. The report tells us that real estate is a busy and growing field. No matter what happens—economic downturns, natural disasters, political upheavals—people will always need a place to live and to raise their families and companies will always need space to house their enterprises and employees. As long as people need protection from the elements, the real estate industry will need bright, principled, hardworking, dynamic, energetic, and service-oriented individuals to help lead folks to owning their own homes and/or businesses. Those who are positive, resourceful, knowledgeable, and prepared, even in this often feast-or-famine pursuit, can weather the roughest storms.

If you are interested in a real estate career, this book is for you. Its key goal is to give you a basic overview and understanding of the field. By presenting facts about various parts of the industry, introducing a wide variety of job choices under the real-estate umbrella, and sharing advice and insights from professionals in the field, our hope is to give you an honest picture of what you will need to bring to the table and what you will find when you arrive. Real estate is not for the timid. It is not for those without entrepreneurial spirit. Knowing the challenges from the outset makes one better placed to surmount the inevitable challenges and to thrive. In short, if you ultimately choose to work in real estate, this book is your guide to putting your best foot forward, to thinking and sounding like a pro from day one, and to maximizing your success.

For those who are prepared for the challenge of starting a new real estate career, this is an excellent time to get going. The housing market is seeing a great deal of volatility at the time of this writing, due to the national and global economic recession. But guess what: the population is still growing. Even in the midst of economic turmoil, families still need homes. Many people are trying their hands at new businesses, and they need space. The wave of home foreclosures that took place in 2008 and 2009 is bad news for families that were displaced. However, this means that even with a decline in new home construction, there are many available properties that must be sold throughout the nation—career opportunities for new real estate professionals.

Data from the Bureau of Labor Statistics supports this. Its latest projection is that employment of real-estate brokers and sales agents should grow 11 percent through 2016. Relatively low interest rates and falling prices should stimulate sales of real estate, says the Bureau, which means more agents and brokers will be needed. Job growth in the industry for support staff may not be as intense, however: tech-savvy agents are more efficient and have less of a need for support staffers, and consumers can now utilize the Internet to do their own research. This does not bode well for part-timers or temporary workers, but full-timers who know the Internet and invest in required technology should thrive. The government also notes that a large number of job openings will arise from the need to replace workers who leave this often fluid industry, where life changes lead some people to enter, leave, and later return to the field.

Even when the market is not ideal, when media outlets report that some "bottom" has been reached, the real estate industry can expand. To call it recession-proof may overstate the case, but when prices soften, certain buyers shy away from shopping for homes, and the amounts of commission checks fall, good buys can be found. Despite the gloom and doom reported by the talking heads on the nightly news, most Americans are employed and do have good credit, plus the interest and wherewithal to buy. For resourceful agents, even in the midst of economic trouble, successful careers can be launched and money can be made in the field of real estate. History bears this out. Since the gradual transition of hunter-gatherer societies to more agrarian communities, the right of homeownership has been of primary concern to human beings. The process of establishing ownership acknowledged and respected by others—be it through might-makes-right arrangements, protection rackets, or the mortgages and deeds we use today—has always been a roller-coaster ride. Understanding the history of real estate enables us to get a better sense of its present and future.

To that end, this book will give you an express trip through the evolution of the modern real estate industry. You will see how the profession has survived peaks and valleys over the years and how it still continues to grow and change. Keep in mind that real estate is more than merely selling houses to families. The industry also includes sales and leasing of properties to government institutions and businesses. Real estate professionals are responsible for managing and renting shopping mall space. Apartment leasing and condominium sales, home and apartment swaps, and sales and leasing of farmland and vacation properties all fall under the real estate category. Many more career opportunities exist as well. This book will outline these and others so you can see the scope of vocational opportunity that exists in this industry.

If you decide to enter the field, we want you to succeed. So do women and men who will be your colleagues and employers. This book includes anecdotes from notable industry veterans and leaders who are very accomplished in the field. By all accounts, they welcome new blood. All were only too happy to offer helpful tips from the trenches. Interestingly, each shared this among the pearls of wisdom they presented: If you want to join their ranks, you must be prepared—academically, emotionally, financially, even spiritually—before you walk into the door of a realty office seeking work. As Diane Honeycutt, self-proclaimed real-estate star of Concord, North Carolina, notes on her "Star Power" blog, "We must train ourselves as world class athletes and grab hold of the drive and determination to be the best in our business we can be."

Chapter 1

Industry History

In the beginning, humans supported their existence by living off the land, finding shelter in caves or under trees as they could, and wandering in search of food. Vulnerable as they were to the elements, wild animals, and other humans, this nomadic lifestyle made long-term survival nearly impossible, and, as one can imagine, it eventually lost its luster. Between 30,000 B.C.E. and 15,000 B.C.E., many humans left hunting and gathering behind, gradually moving into agriculture-centered lives. This is the point in history where the concept of real estate—owning one's own land—essentially came into being.

In these primitive times, the means of establishing land-ownership were very rudimentary. As business writer Andrew Beattie puts it in the Investopedia article "No Longer Nomads": "Fertile plains were staked out and settled in a might-makes-right manner in which those who could defend the land were those who kept it." Real estate writer Lloyd Duhaime puts it more succinctly: "You had it, you owned it. You wanted it, you fought for it. You found it, you kept it." The strongest man or group of men of a particular tribe would appoint themselves the leaders of those around them. One of their tasks as rulers was to choose who could live on what piece of land. Often, they would retain ownership for themselves. Leaders exacted payment for the favor of dispersing land, and as wealth grew and communities evolved, empires expanded. As Beattie writes:

> The shift toward more and more powerful tribal leaders culminated in a pooling of labor along with a CEO of sorts to direct efforts.

Irrigation channels were dug, strongholds were built, farming methods improved and temples were erected. With the land improvement, populations also exploded. Now, where a family of hunter-gatherers might be able to support one or two children at best, farmers could produce several children. The increased fertility also meant increased available laborers.

As centuries passed and populations grew exponentially, armies became necessary to thwart invaders from other areas. This created what Beattie refers to as "the original protection racket": People who tacitly agreed to serve, obey, and pay taxes to the leaders—ultimately called emperors, pharaohs, chiefs, or kings—so that their land would be protected. At the same time, resourceful citizens had a means for earning wealth for themselves as well. Those with talents in the arts or in skills such as masonry and carpentry could market their own labor, crafts, and creations. Those with entrepreneurial instincts and business acumen could trade items in the marketplace. This created a class of merchants, which led to real estate as we know it. The leader may have owned the land, but merchants could lay claim to (and build, buy, rent, and sell) the houses on top of the land.

Over the centuries, even as civilizations adopted more humane philosophies, the prevailing idea of legal systems was "might makes right." This concept was writ large in 1066, when the Normans conquered England and Norman leader William declared that, by right of conquest, every inch of the country was his. Ironically, by assuming ownership of England, he reduced the need for others to fight among themselves. As British nobility expert and author Paul M. Remfry notes on the Castle Wales Web site, "It had been possible during his reign for a man to walk with his pockets full of gold from one end of William's realm to the other with no one touching him through their fear of the king."

King William the Conqueror used more than fear to inspire loyalty. He further secured his position as monarch by giving parcels of land to his Norman soldiers, to his favored friends, to traveling knights, and to titled English families willing to recognize him as king. Land bestowed power and access in William's court. Land meant wealth, and social class was determined by the amount of land in one's control. That control went only so far, however. Since all land was ultimately owned by the king, he could reclaim all land given to others at any time.

Fast
Facts

On Home Loans

The word *mortgage* comes from the French legal term meaning "dead pledge." A mortgage is a conditional arrangement that stipulates the obligations of the lien holder and the buyer; in other words, it details what will happen if one does not repay the loan according to the accepted terms of the contract. Old English law instituted three states of ownership:

Fee tail: Under English law, the tenant could bequeath land to a direct descendant, such as a natural child, under this type of ownership.

Life estate: This ownership tenure lasted only until the tenant's death, after which tenancy went back to the lord.

Fee simple: This, the most extensive form of ownership, allowed the tenant to sell or transfer property to an heir if the tenant died without a legal will in force. In real estate today, almost all land bought and sold via mortgages falls under this category, which is as close as one can get to complete ownership as one can have acknowledged under law.

King William's practices of land dispersal gradually mutated into what was known as a feudal system. This was a governing system based on obligations between a lord and his favored associates, or vassals. Under the system, the king gave large estates and promises of protection to his relatives and vassals. These estates (the "fiefs") included buildings, tools, livestock, and laborers (also known as serfs). In return, those who managed the fiefs vowed military service and loyalty to the king in all things. Whatever the king requested—money, lodging, manpower, soldiers, companionship—they had to provide. Their favored position in society, no doubt, made the currying worthwhile. The arrangement resembled a modern-day Ponzi scheme: The king (an olden-day Bernie Madoff) was at the top of the pyramid, with descending levels of subdivisions underneath, each headed by its own lord. By the twelfth century, the feudal model was prevalent throughout much of Western Europe.

The rise of the feudal system brought with it new divisions among classes. Beneath the king and the lords, fiefs were a series of ranks of lower vassals who pledged loyalty to the lords in exchange for a piece of land to call their own. Below them were the freemen peasants, tradesmen, and artisans who paid fees to rent land from the lord. They were able to keep a portion of the crops for food and a portion was paid to the lord. At the lowest level below the freemen were the serfs, who were mandated to serve the upper classes and in the military. They were forced to pay taxes to their lord and to the king for their meager living conditions. If ownership of land was transferred from one lord to another, so was ownership of the serfs. To offer some perspective, roughly 90 percent of the population filled the serf class. All peasants were required to pay rent to the lord, in the form of grain, honey, and eggs that the peasant raised on his plot of land.

As the systems of societal organization were still in flux, so were the legal systems that governed them. At the foundation of Western law was the Magna Carta, a feudal charter of liberties issued by King John of England in 1215. This document, which influenced the United States' own founding documents, covers numerous topics including estate law. One of the major sections defines "escheat," a condition whereby control of land reverts back from the deceased tenant to the lord. If a tenant died without heirs or pleaded guilty committing a felony, escheat went into effect; otherwise, control was passed on to surviving relatives. The law also defined different types of tenancy, also called tenures or estates, some of which still remain in use today. For example, freehold tenancy meant the tenant was a freeman who had rights the non-freeman did not. Non-freehold tenants were called copyhold, tenancy at will, or tenancy for a fixed period. Tenancy for a fixed period is still in effect today.

The statutes of estate law as defined by the Magna Carta were extended by the Statute Quia Emptores, an English law which passed in 1290, forbidding tenant A from granting a part of his land to tenant B and becoming tenant B's lord. It slowed the feudalistic Ponzi scheme by banning further subdivision of lands, save by the king. It also permitted tenants to sell their land rights without having to secure prior permission from the lord. Eventually, the fief system faded, leaving a free market to facilitate the buying and selling of land. By the end of the medieval period, laws had passed which allowed vassals (lords and other noblemen) to pay large sums of money to the king for outright ownership of the land.

The English legal system, exported to lands including Australia and New Zealand, was the basis for much of the commerce that took place in the world over the next several centuries. Over time, the power of most royals was made extinct or else rendered purely ornamental; governments—some elected, some not—made decisions for societies. This was the template followed by the English colonies that declared themselves a sovereign nation in 1776. In the 1800s, the still-young United States was evolving into a land aspiring to liberty for all, and such aspirations would affect the national approach to property management for years to come.

Throughout its first century of existence, the U.S. economy was primarily agricultural. With the advent of the Industrial Revolution in the early-to-mid-1800s, everything changed as competition and speed become the order of the day. Mass production forced artisans out of business because they could not keep up with the accelerated pace set by factories, thus driving them into cities for factory and office jobs. The same fate awaited some farmers who lost business to growers with access to automated machines. This boom of industrial labor led to the rise of the middle class—those who work for someone else to secure a better life for their families. Workers were able to earn more income than through farming or working on others' farms, and had more disposable income. Since part of raising a family means securing shelter—either renting a dwelling or buying a home—the field of real estate began to take a greater place in the national economy.

Of course, real estate was a thriving industry in the United States long before the Industrial Revolution. When the Revolutionary War ended, the brand new federal government sold or granted one billion acres of land to private owners and land grants. Land grants (selling of land for little or no money) were made by the government so the grantees could build railroads, highways, or colleges. This occurred throughout the successive decades. In the mid-1800s, a federal land sale sold 20 million acres for about $1.25 per acre—a price most Americans could not afford. Activists stepped up to speak for the people. The Free Soil Movement was founded to ask the government to create a method that would allow more citizens to enter the ranks of homeownership. The grassroots effort worked: Congress passed the Homestead Act of 1862, which gave citizens 160 acres for every adult in the household. In exchange, the owners would live on and work the land for at least five years. This distribution plan worked so well that similar programs sprung up through the late 1800s, as the nation's economy shifted from primarily agricultural to increasingly industrial. By the end, more than 300 million acres of public property were in the hands of citizens who were free to transfer title to their land via sale, rental, or trade. This was the foundation of the modern real estate system.

By the turn of the nineteenth century, mortgages had entered the scene in a very big way. Yet they were not a new concept. Kings and other wealthy landowners had for centuries permitted their friends to purchase land through a loan arrangement that sometimes included "interest," an additional fee to pay for the privilege of receiving the loan. The sudden growth of cities brought the mortgage loan to regular people. Banks were able to provide funding for people who wished to buy homes and earn additional revenue in the

Fast Facts

Behind the Wall Street Crash of 1929

Looking at the reasons behind the stock market crash of 1929 can offer some insight into the economic challenges we face today. Until the 1920s, stock market trading was limited to professionals. During that decade, however, rules were relaxed to allow participation by regular citizens. This led to a speculative boom: hundreds of thousands of Americans with dollar signs in their eyes began to invest heavily in the stock market, even as real estate values were in decline. Many people even borrowed money to allow them to purchase more shares of stock. By August 1929, it was not unusual for some brokers to lend small investors more than two-thirds of the face value of the stocks they were buying. More than $8.5 billion was out on loan, a figure some speculate exceeded the entire amount of currency circulating throughout the country. Stock prices rose, so more people leapt into the market, which pushed prices to heights they had never seen before. This caused an economic bubble, and on October 24, 1929, the market fell nearly 20 percent, triggering a national panic in which shareholders started selling their stocks at alarming rates.

interest they paid. Suddenly, normal folks could live in homes while paying for them, knowing that in 10 to 30 years it would be theirs outright. Down the line, the family home could be passed on to future generations, creating strong long-term family units and stable societies. Home ownership became an important part of a good life and a symbol of the middle-class American dream.

By the beginning of the twentieth century, cities were booming. Chicago, the king of Midwestern industry, grew from a population of less than 1,000 in 1830 to 1,698,575 a mere 70 years later! Now the world's fifth and nation's second largest city, its property values skyrocketed accordingly. Similarly, New York boasted 202,589 residents in 1930; in 1900, the U.S. Census bureau reported that the most populous city in the United States had 3,437,202 people living within its five boroughs. By 1920, half of the American population lived in urban settings. This meant many opportunities for developing real estate properties to serve city residents—single-family homes, apartment buildings, office spaces, factories, hotels, restaurants, retail structures, and municipal headquarters. Rising prices made city life very expensive, so many people took advantage of the rising car culture and moved into new communities outside urban centers, the suburbs. The growth of the suburbs provided additional opportunities for the real estate industry, as did the expansion of electric service, the invention of the elevator, and the development of the city skyscraper. Almost everywhere one looked, there was prosperity. Certainly there were many who were poorer than others, but on the whole, the American dream was becoming a beautiful reality for many U.S. citizens.

The Wall Street crash of 1929 changed everything. The United States lurched into an economic depression that lasted roughly a decade. Most American industries—including real estate—were decimated. The mortgage system and financial markets collapsed. Under President Franklin D. Roosevelt, the federal government instituted the New Deal, a massive rescue plan that overhauled Wall Street and infused the real estate financing market with funds to stimulate home sales. One of its crown jewels was the Federal Housing Administration. Founded in 1930, the FHA provided mortgage insurance, which reduced risk for savings and loans, banks, and other lending institutions. Another prime part of the New Deal was the Federal Home Loan Bank System, whose job was to oversee and regulate local banks. In 1934, mortgages began to be widely used again, and the FHA helped lower down payments, making it easier for some

Americans to purchase a home. The Federal National Mortgage Association, otherwise known as Fannie Mae, came on the scene four years later. Fannie Mae was designed to provide an alternate path to home financing for prospective buyers who may not be able to secure traditional bank mortgages. The association also brought investment capital into the mortgage market, a role it still plays today.

The Great Depression, in many ways the worst financial nightmare yet encountered, was far from the last challenge faced by the U.S. real estate industry. Just when the nation was back on the financial upswing, America entered World War II. The ensuing war effort brought real estate development largely to a halt. However, after the victories of 1945, the rise began again. Johnny came marching home, and suddenly the housing market started a brand-new boom. Just one year later, new housing construction rose four times to more than half a million homes, most built in the suburbs. This expansion brought with it new roads and highways, hotel and restaurant chains, fast food, suburban retail shopping malls and movie theaters, and more.

This suburban growth left cities in decline, which led to the rise of community activism. In 1965, grassroots action on behalf of poor and neglected urban populations spurred the establishment of a new cabinet-level department devoted to city housing, known today as the Department of Housing and Urban Development (HUD). Thanks to the efforts of HUD, new commercial and retail buildings were erected between the late 1960s and 2000 intended for the tourism, hospitality, and service industries.

By the late 1980s and early 1990s, the U.S. Congress loosened regulatory control over the financial markets and banks, setting off massive growth on Wall Street and in corporate America. Government programs emerged (along with special mortgage loans from the private sector) that made credit more accessible and home ownership possible for thousands of working-class people who could not previously afford a home. Numerous urban centers benefited from gentrification and home buying, the growth of niche markets (real estate professionals who focus on particular customer bases, such as Christian households, Spanish-speaking buyers, or gay- and lesbian-headed families), and cultural fare generally found in downtown centers. Poverty, crime, and crumbling infrastructure, however, remained pressing challenges for the nation's major cities.

Though deregulation opened up channels of homeownership previously inaccessible to the majority of Americans, it was not

Everyone

....➤

Knows

The Costs of Becoming a Real Estate Agent

You do not decide to become a real estate agent one day and find a job and become one the next. To become a real estate agent you must first obtain a license. That may mean taking state approved classes which can cost upwards of $200–$300 or more. Books will add to that figure. Then there is the cost for the license itself. It varies from state to state, so check with your state licensing agency to find out how much it is in your state. However, individuals can expect to spend as much as $100 for a license. Some real estate firms offer pre-licensing classes to their agents who are studying to obtain their licenses.

Once you are licensed your out-of-pocket expenses may not be over. Many real estate companies do not provide marketing and advertising material to their agents. Agents are expected to pay for their own business cards and brochures. Talk to other agents working for real estate firms you are interested in joining. Find out how much out-of-pocket expenses you may have before you join.

without its negative ramifications. Before deregulation, a prospective homebuyer needed to demonstrate a strong financial foundation. The process was exhausting and the qualifications a buyer was required to meet were strict. Prospects had to prove that they could afford a down payment and were fiscally stable enough to manage the responsibility of paying the monthly mortgage fee. If the lender was satisfied that the candidate was worthy, the sale would go through. People who truly could not afford to buy homes did not buy homes.

This changed with deregulation. Initially, when lawmakers loosened laws governing financial institutions and interest rates dropped, business boomed. To take advantage of this, the banking industry invented new and sophisticated investment instruments such as Collateralized Debt Obligation, which allows spreading around the risk in real estate loans. These instruments were marketed to other financial institutions, among them Fannie Mae and

---

INTERVIEW

A Veteran's Perspective

Walter Hall
Chairman of HouseSavvy, USA, LLC

How did you get started in real estate?

I started after leaving the service. Started a residential business in 1960 and built it into one of the largest agencies in New England. It was a multifaceted operation with lots of agents. In 1978, we segued a training division into the Hall Institute of Real Estate. We were hired by top realtors throughout the country for training and management development programs. The Institute helped state realty associations in all 50 states. My next effort, which lasted from 1978 to 2003, segued that into Relocation Resources International, a real estate brokerage that offered training and financial expertise in global relocation. We processed 10,000 to 13,000 relocating homeowners yearly around the world. For many years, I had a dream that there was a better business model than the current one (one size fits all for 5 or 6 percent commission).

What did you learn from all this research and testing?

We dealt with hundreds of sellers and buyers over four years and found that they wanted more: more choices, more reasonably priced services, more flexibility and involvement. People wanted access to information previously restricted to real estate professionals. The needs we found showed a need for an online service, and out of that, HouseSavvy evolved.

This is different from what customers needed before?

That is right. Today's prospective buyers do have a different set of needs than prior generations. Now, people know more and our industry is less mysterious. Buyers today want more involvement and 24/7 access to service. That is how we have seen the industry change, though it has been a gradual change, a trending in that direction, not an avalanche.

So, in the present recessionary market and with a more knowledgeable and demanding customer base, what is the best way for real estate pros to survive?

They have to know themselves, their strengths, their personalities. Personal inventory-taking helps to know what you do well and where you fall short. The Hall Institute taught to keep separate designations for listing agents, selling agents, and buyer agents. The best agents were those who had could balance empathy and ego-drive. You need a good balance. Ego-drive: you cannot sell without it, but too much can turn people off. Empathy in a sales situation can turn to sympathy, [which is] not good. Empathetic [people] are great listing agents, though, because they listen, call their customers, comfort and console them, and hold their hands.

It is rare that we found both qualities in the same people, and we worked with thousands of agents. It is rare to find a strong listing agent who is also a strong selling agent. Eighty percent of the money is brought in by 20 percent of the agents. In this economy, it is closer to 90/10. Sheer economics is getting rid of and weeding out underperformers.

Looking at what we have learned from the history, we see the future of real estate heading where we are heading: You provide viable service based on knowledge and technological applications. You need good sellers and good listings. Listing is everything. That has not changed.

What do you wish you had known when you started in this business?
I was about 25 when I started. It took four years to realize that to be successful, you had to control the merchandise, have the most listings. I wish I had known to deal only with motivated buyers and not with people who are just kicking the tires. They are wasting your time, and today, there is no time to waste. On the other side, everything is motivation in real estate. With some buyers, it would take four or five years to ask the key questions to find if they were worthy leads.

How is the recession affecting your work?
I have seen a positive trend in Boston since January. Historically, there are three measurements of a real estate market's health: sales activity; average sales price; and the key one, unsold home inventory. At the national level, there is an average nine-month supply of unsold homes. To find that figure, you find the number of unsold listings at the end of a month, then the number of sales during that month. Divide the number of sales into the number of unsold listings, and that gives you the current rate of sales.

A nine-month supply? Has it always been that way?
We used to assume a six-month supply was indicative of a balanced market. That changes in a volatile market, so it is certainly different now. That is always a thing in real estate that is hard to convey in the

(continued on next page)

INTERVIEW

A Veteran's Perspective (continued)

national angle. Industry types talk about Las Vegas, Florida, Miami condominiums, the Rust Belt, and Detroit. A lot of markets were not hurt that badly by the economic fallout and do not have a lot of foreclosure or sub-prime markets. The old axiom goes, "What goes up fast, comes down fast." If you look at statistics, Las Vegas went bananas, [but] it had an equal and opposite decline in the speed of dollars. Speed of [increase] matched speed of [decline]. Nationally, the picture is different, but overall, things are not as bad as they seem.

So what is your advice for newbies in light of all this?
One: Be able to carry yourself financially for at least a year and a half. There is nothing available in residential real estate (other than clerical work) that involves salary. It is all commission. Even if you are successful, you will not see cash for months. It is always forward revenue. Understanding that is the single most important thing today other than skills and personality. Two: Go into it with your eyes open. Talk to people who are successful agents and pick their brains. Find people

the Federal Home Loan Mortgage Corporation (Freddie Mac), the congressionally chartered, shareholder-owned companies that provide most of the nation's home mortgage funds. The combination of falling interest rates, easy credit, and deregulation led many banks to make home loans to thousands of individuals whose applications previously would have been rejected. Still, banks went forward, assuming much of the risk would fall to Fannie Mae and Freddie Mac. The Macs, for their part, repackaged the loans and sold them to other banks, which in turn re-bundled the loans yet again and sold them to pension funds, private investors, and other global investment companies. Then, interest rates began to rise. Many of those initial home loans—shaky from the outset—went bad as homeowners across the country realized they could not make their mortgage payments. No, it was not the Great Crash of 1929 again, but it was a bloodbath. The American financial house of cards tumbled, creating who just left the industry—talk to them and get their perceptions. Three: Search out historical Multiple Listing Service data sources by calendar quarter. You want to know how many sales have been made per month or quarter so you can actually see what the opportunity is. Then go through MLS data to find out how many active agents are in your area presently. Divide the number of sales by year by the number of active agents. The picture you will see is a very discouraging one, but it will be an honest picture.

What is the main problem that new agents run into when they enter the field?
Experienced real estate agents do not tell them the truth! For instance, yes, we go to parties, go to conventions, and have a lot of fun, but you do not set your own hours. Real estate careers make you work more hours than almost any field out there. Also, people get into this saying they are going to "do real estate." There is a big difference between "doing real estate" and having a real estate career. Lots of people have a real estate license. They might dabble in it once or twice. That is doing real estate, but that is not a career.

Another thing: Sixty percent of new agents bail within a year. Why? The money. They cannot deal with the commission aspect. The average realtor only makes $42,000 per year, and that is with no perks, no life insurance, no health coverage, no dental. If they are not in love with selling real estate, if they are not willing to make it a real career, they might as well work [somewhere else].

an economic disaster affecting nearly every industry in the country and industrial nations around the world.

A Brief Chronology

15,000 B.C.E.: Humans become farmers rather than hunters and gatherers, making land valuable.

1066 A.D.: The Normans conquer England and claim ownership of the land through right of conquest.

1200: Feudal system is developed in Europe.

1215: The Magna Carta is written and made law. It contains many real estate directives still in use today.

1290: The Statute Quia Emptores becomes English Law. It keeps tenants from subleasing their land and becoming the lords of other tenants.

1776: The United States declares its independence from the British.

1783: At the end of the Revolutionary War the new American government sells one billion acres of land to private owners.

1800s: The industrial revolution causes people to migrate from the country to cities. Workers acquire more income and the middle class begins to form.

1862: Congress passes the Homestead Act, which gave citizens 160 acres for every adult in the household.

1900s: Mortgages become more common and allow people of all economic backgrounds to purchase their own homes.

1920: Half of the American population lives in urban settings.

1929: The stock market crash precipitates the Great Depression. Real estate development comes to a halt until after World War II.

1945: The economy and the real estate industry begin to boom following World War II.

1965: The Department of Housing and Urban Development is developed in response to the phenomenal growth of suburbs and the decline of urban centers. Its goal is to assist the revitalization of urban areas.

1990s: The U.S. Congress loosens regulatory control over the financial markets and banks, setting off massive growth on Wall Street and in corporate America. Government programs emerge (along with special mortgage loans from the private sector) that make credit more accessible and homeownership possible for thousands of working-class people who could not previously afford a home.

2000s: Loosening regulatory control leads to banks granting loans to applicants who could not have previously afforded a home. Thousands of borrowers' mortgages go into default: they owe more on their homes than the homes are worth.

2008: The Emergency Economic Stabilization Act of 2008 is passed into law. It authorizes the United States government to spend up $700 billion to purchase distressed assets, especially mortgage-backed securities, and make capital injections into banks.

Chapter 2

State of the Industry

The real estate industry has seen its share of ups and downs in its very long history. From being owned by one king, to disbursement to vassals, and eventually the ability for the "common" person to buy a home through obtaining a mortgage, real estate has been the stuff of people's dreams. Owning one's own home is a traditional American aspiration, and that has not changed. Despite the problems with the economy and recent downturn in the real estate market and home values, people still need a roof over their heads. Homes are still moving. You still see "For Sale" signs in people's yards, and very often "Sold" signs as well. Existing home sales fell in January 2010 (from December 2009), but were still above January 2009 levels, according to the National Association of Realtors. Such statistics indicate a noticeable upswing.

Unfortunately, the commercial real estate segment is still struggling, and experts forecast a sluggish recovery throughout 2010. Major office markets in Boston are offering tenants free rent of up to six months. Even in Manhattan, free rent deals go up to more than four months. Still, the outlook is not all gloom and doom. The need for housing, office, and retail space will always be there, and as the economy recovers, so will these markets.

There is a marked difference, however, between residential and commercial realtors' confidence in a market recovery. In October 2009, the National Association of Realtors surveyed commercial realtors about the business in their markets. Most responded pessimistically, with more than 50 percent citing financing as their biggest stumbling block. Residential realtors, on the other hand, say they are seeing noticeable improvements in home sales in their markets from the previous year. They cite specifically the improvement of indexes for townhouses and condos. Realtors in some areas are more confident than others. According to the National Association of Realtors, those in the western United States are much more confident than all of the other regions, while the least confident region is the Midwest.

The good news is that 61 percent of residential real estate agents participated in the sale of a home in January 2010. However, 68 percent of those sales were buyers purchasing a vacant home. Financing did not appear to be the same problem it was for commercial realtors. The realtors participating in the National Association of Realtors survey reported that 37 percent of their buyers only needed a down payment of 3 to 6 percent of the purchase price. Fifteen percent of buyers did not make a down payment at all, while 21 percent paid the more standard down payment of 11 to 20 percent. Within the residential real estate market, the single-family homes segment appears to be faring the best. Distressed property sales (homes that are in foreclosure or short sales) rose from 32 percent of home sales in January 2009 to 38 percent of home sales in January 2010. This indicates that a great number of residential home sales are still distressed properties.

The Challenges Ahead

Both residential and commercial real estate professionals face many challenges in the coming years. Financing continues to be a challenge. Lending institutions are enacting tougher qualification standards, making it harder for individuals and businesses to get the financing they need. Another challenge facing both residential and commercial markets is unemployment. Although unemployment is expected to decline in the last half of 2010, it is still in the double digits, which means there will be fewer people making moves and fewer employers adding staff and needing larger office space. In fact, some may still be downsizing. This does not bode well for either residential or commercial realtors.

A big challenge specific to the residential real estate industry continues to be the sale of distressed properties. The wait for banks to approve short sales, in addition to the paperwork processing that must be completed before closing, has a negative effect on home sales. Many home buyers wait months for a bank to respond to their offer and walk away from the deal before the bank is able to close. While the government and many banks are working to streamline this process, residential realtors will continue to find this a challenging aspect of their jobs.

No one can deny the impact the current economy is having on all segments of the real estate industry. The current economic climate is more hopeful than in the last few years, but still challenging for real estate professionals as they seek to deal with the aftermath of the recent upheaval. Realtors and others in the industry will need to be creative and find ways to adapt in this more challenging economic climate.

Employment, Wages, and Profits

The real estate industry is one of the larger industries in the United States, and there are many jobs available for those who wish to embark on a real estate career. According to the U.S. Bureau of Labor Statistics, real estate brokers and sales agents held about 517,800 jobs in 2008. Real estate sales agents represent the lion's share of these jobs, holding approximately 76 percent. Although there are many other industry-related jobs, such as mortgage bankers, real estate appraisers, property managers, and home inspectors, most real estate professionals are agents, brokers, or work for agents or brokers.

The good news is that despite the recent downturn in the economy, the number of real estate broker and agent jobs is expected to grow in the next several years, and at a pace faster than the average of all jobs tracked by the U.S. Bureau of Labor Statistics. This may seem somewhat counterintuitive to current market conditions. However, the Bureau says employment of real estate brokers and sales agents is expected to grow 14 percent by 2018. This relatively high growth rate will be the result of a growing population of young couples and individuals looking to buy homes, many who will be first time home buyers.

According to the Bureau, a large number of job openings will arise from the need to replace workers who transfer to other occupations or leave the labor force. The Bureau reports that the current population of real estate brokers and sales agents consists of older workers, on average, than most other professions, and many are expected to leave the occupation over the next decade. Additionally, the slow economy has caused many real estate professionals to change careers.

Fast
Facts

Job Growth in the Real Estate Industry

Looking at the eight professions below, and the projected growth in the number of jobs by the year 2018, it is clear to see that professionals in the design, construction, and inspection of homes will see the biggest growth. The slowest growth will be in administrative jobs, like loan processors.

1. Agents and brokers, 14% growth
2. Appraisers and assessors, 5% growth
3. Architects, 16% growth
4. Home inspectors, 17% growth
5. Landscape architects, 20% growth
6. Loan interviewers and clerks, 4% growth
7. Mortgage Loan Officers, 10% growth
8. Property managers, 8% growth

Source: U.S. Bureau of Labor Statistics

There are some parts of the country where real estate agents may be more successful finding jobs and selling properties. According to data gathered and reported by the National Association of Realtors as of January 2010, home sales in the western United States continue to do better than in other parts of the country. Another region of the country where home sales appear to be doing better is the northeast. Agents who relocate to these areas of the country may have a better chance of success than those in the other areas of the United States.

When it comes to earnings, real estate agents' and brokers' salaries are primarily comprised of commission, either of their own sales or the sales of the other agents in their firms. Because the economy has created a slower than average real estate market, the annual earnings for real estate professionals has not grown in the last few years. Some professionals saw a decline while others were able to hold their own.

According to government statistics available at the U.S. Bureau of Labor Statistics Web site, the average annual salary of real estate sales agents was $40,150 as of May 2008. The middle 50 percent earned between $27,390 and $64,820 a year. The lowest 10 percent earned less than $21,120, and the highest 10 percent earned more than $101,860. Some segments of the real estate industry fared better than others. Despite the fact that new construction of residential homes decreased, real estate agents in the new home construction segment earned an additional $5,000 in income over the next top earner, agents in the land subdivision segment. Real estate agents working in the leasing segment of the industry earned the smallest salary.

The average annual wages for real estate brokers, on the other hand, were $57,500 in May 2008. The middle 50 percent earned between $36,420 and $93,970 a year. Similar to agents, brokers in some real estate market segments earned higher salaries than those in others. Again, the top earning brokers were in the residential building segment. They earned an average of $63,280. The next highest earning segment, brokers in real estate offices, earned an average yearly salary of $59,710. The brokers who reported earning the least in 2008 were those in the real estate leasing segment of the industry.

Keep in mind that agents and brokers may have to split or share their commissions in a few situations. For example, if one agent sells a home another agent has listed, the typical 6 percent commission is divided between the selling and buying agents. Most agents must also pay a percentage of their commissions to their broker or the real estate firm they work for. In addition, since the agent usually pays for his or her own marketing and advertising tools, his or her net income may be somewhat reduced after these expenses are deducted from the agent's salary.

Current Trends

When it comes to current trends in the real estate industry, one in particular stands out in the minds of most real estate professionals: distressed home sales. In fact, according to information gathered and reported by the National Association of Realtors, short sales can make up more than a third of all home sales in the United States.

There are three primary types of distressed home sales: short sales, foreclosures, and deeds in lieu of foreclosure. Short sales occur when the homeowner is selling a property and the current market value is less than he or she owes on the mortgage. There are many reasons why short sales are prevalent in the market today. One of the most prominent reasons is that many regions in the country overbuilt during the economic boom of the early 2000s, building more homes than the demand for them in that area. Thus the homes' values declined rather than increased. Another primary reason there are so many short sales is that many banks and other lenders financed a larger than usual percentage of the home's appraised value, sometimes up to 100 percent. When the bottom fell out of the economy and unemployment rose, the real estate market declined and home values plummeted. Home owners found themselves owing more on their homes than they were worth in the new market conditions.

Foreclosures are also occurring nearly as often as short sales. Foreclosures occur when borrowers no longer make mortgage payments. After several attempts to collect the money owed, the bank forecloses, taking ownership of the property. Once the bank forecloses it will put the property up for sale in an effort to recover the money the delinquent borrower owed. Foreclosures can negatively impact a homeowner's credit report.

The third option economically challenged homeowners can choose is to voluntarily turn over the deed (and all other assets used as collateral to finance the home) to the bank in lieu of foreclosure. In this option the bank still ends up owning the property and attempting to sell it, but homeowners' credit reports do not reflect a foreclosure. In many states, if the bank is unable to sell the property at a price that allows it to recover the amount the borrower owes, the borrower is responsible for the difference and the bank can take legal action to acquire the money. In a deed in lieu of foreclosure, the bank agrees that it will accept the deed and all other assets used as collateral as full payment. The borrower's debt is then forgiven.

As already mentioned, distressed home sales are not only a current trend, but a growing one, and one that can frustrate the real estate professional. This is because the bank has now entered the negotiations, and sale prices and conditions must meet their approval before a sale can occur. In short sales the real estate agent, buyer, and seller negotiate a sale price. Once the buyer and seller agree on a price, there are documents that need to be submitted to the bank for the bank's approval. The bank can take up to two to three months— sometimes even longer—before letting the seller know it has agreed to the buyer's offer. The result is that buyers often cannot wait for this bureaucratic system to slowly perform its duties for many different reasons: Perhaps they have already sold a home and need a new one to move into. Or maybe they have been renting and must move when the lease ends. For whatever reason, many buyers walk away from a home and deal they are happy with, and the seller has to start all over finding a buyer. There is also no guarantee at the end of the waiting period that the bank will approve the sale price. When it is not approved the seller must either renegotiate with the original buyer or find a new buyer and start all over.

Foreclosures can be equally frustrating to deal with for buyers and real estate professionals. It is usually harder to negotiate a sale price with a bank, which is looking more at the money it must recover than the current market value of the home. Also, if there is damage to the home, the seller is usually responsible for repairing it. When the bank owns the home, it may choose to sell it "as is" rather than paying for repairs. All of this can drive away the prospective buyer.

The good news is that the government, recognizing that distressed home sales is a growing and frustrating trend in the residential home sales market, implemented the Home Affordable Foreclosure Alternatives (HAFA) Program in April of 2010. Part of the Home Affordable Modification Program (HAMP), HAFA helps homeowners who are unable to retain their home under HAMP by simplifying and streamlining the use of short sales and deeds in lieu of foreclosures. However, not all homeowners will qualify or be able to utilize this program. As we enter the second decade of the twenty-first century, it is clear that economic recovery is on the horizon. However, it is slower than predicted, and the number of distressed home sales will continue to be a very big trend in the real estate industry for the next several years.

Going hand-in-hand with distressed home sales, the second biggest trend real estate professionals in the residential industry will see is an increasing number of first time buyers. With home values hitting very low levels, homes are now more affordable for the first time buyer. These buyers will be flooding the residential market because of the opportunities presented by lowered property values and government tax incentives, such as the first time buyer tax incentive of an $8,000 credit. As the market recovers, he or she will realize very strong returns on his or her investment. First time buyers are also taking advantage of foreclosures. Interest rates are also still very low, which make home buying more attractive for all buyers, but especially the first time buyer.

The final major trend that will continue to play a role in the next several years is a tightening on the availability of financing. This trend holds true for both residential and commercial real estate markets. Mortgage banks, commercial banks, and other lenders have tightened their guidelines and offerings and many buyers are having trouble acquiring the financing they need to make a real estate purchase. For example, it was once common for a buyer to be able to finance 100 percent of his loan. Now it is rare to find a lender that still offers this product. Lenders are once again requiring larger down payments and using stricter income guidelines. Businesses are finding financing even harder to come by than prospective buyers, making leasing or subleasing space their only alternatives.

Technology

For the last 15 to 20 years, technology has been impacting just about every facet of the real estate industry, whether you are an agent, broker, buyer, or seller. The technology that has had the biggest impact, especially in the residential market, has been the Internet. Beginning in the 1990s multiple listing service (MLS) sites began publishing all listings in easily searchable databases. For example, if you were interested in a home in a particular city you could search the database using the city's zip codes. You could then narrow this list of homes even further by searching for homes in a specific price range, or by the number of bedrooms and bathrooms you were looking for.

Prior to this time, people interested in finding a home could only look at listings through a real estate agent. The potential buyer called an agent, set up an appointment, and looked through listings in a book. The listings provided basic information about the home, such as the year it was built, square footage, and the number of bedrooms and bathrooms it had. It also displayed one or two pictures of the exterior. The buyer would choose a few listings from the book to go visit, or bypass the book and let the realtor choose the properties for him or her to view. The potential buyer relied on the realtor to tell him or her what the fair market value of a property was, and whether the asking price was comparable to similar homes in the area.

When Web sites began publishing MLS listings, the information about the homes stayed the same, but over time realtors began putting more pictures of the property on the Internet. Buyers could see eight to 10 photos, most of them of the inside of a home, from the comfort of their living rooms. They could rule out properties without having to spend the time to go see them, as well as have access to most of the information they needed to know when considering the home, such as estimated taxes and even the estimated house payment based on common available interest rates. Both buyers and sellers could view all of the listings in their area and know the asking prices of all the homes. They could calculate what might work as an asking price for their home, or what a reasonable offer would be on a home they were interested in buying. Potential buyers became more educated about homes, their values, and the buying process.

With this, the real estate agent's job began to change. Instead of spending a great deal of time sorting through listings and creating a list of homes to view with a buyer, buyers were calling an agent with their list of homes they wanted to visit. Agents and brokers began spending less time educating their clients, but more time defending a suggested sale or asking price. It became important for agents to provide several good quality photos of a property in order to attract potential buyers.

Keeping
in Touch

Social Networks

Real estate professionals are just beginning to understand why using social and professional networks like Facebook, Twitter, and LinkedIn can lead to new sales leads or increased business.

There are a number of reasons why professionals are now jumping into the social network bandwagon with both feet. Most of the reasons tie back to the most important one: the end result. If used correctly, social networks produce the kind of results most sales professionals and businesses are looking for, and at the lowest price possible. Signing up is free.

To get the most out of your social network, you need to post regular, informative status reports, about the market in general, your recent successes, or ideas for making the most of current trends. Your network friends "tuning in" will soon be impressed with your knowledge and expertise and either call on you for their real estate needs or recommend you to others.

The interiors of listing homes needed to be staged for the photos and home visits to look as spacious as possible. As time went on, videos of properties were added along with photos. If an agent was working with a buyer, he or she had to become more knowledgeable about current market values of homes sold in the immediate area, how long they had been on the market, and how to help the buyer obtain financing. If the agent was working with a seller, he or she had to become an expert in marketing, especially Internet marketing. Today, fewer agents and brokers use newspapers and television ads to advertise listings. Former television "home shows" are now broadcast on a real estate company's Web site, where viewers can watch them 24/7. More real estate companies are using videos such as these to market their listings.

Another impact technology has made on the industry is in agent response time. Before the Internet and e-mail, clients would contact a realtor and expect a response in the next day or two. Thanks to the Internet and cell phones, real estate agents are now "on call" 24 hours a day. Clients can call an agent's cell phone or e-mail him or her at any hour of the day or night and expect to receive a response. This is especially true today when many agents have Blackberries, iPhones, and other advanced cell phones with Internet access. Beyond improving communications, the Internet has also become a valuable tool for realtors to develop new client relationships through social and business networking sites such as LinkedIn, Facebook, and MySpace. Realtors are also writing and posting articles and blogs to establish their credibility as real estate agents. These blogs help them develop relationships with potential clients who read them and then seek to communicate with their authors.

Another major technology change that is becoming prevalent in the real estate industry is the use of Web-based business applications. Previously, these applications were installed on the agent's computer or the company's server, taking up a lot of hard drive space. Now some agents, brokers, or real estate companies pay subscription fees to access their programs online. The main advantage, in addition to saving hard drive space, is that they are available anytime and anywhere the agent or user needs them.

Key Conferences and Industry Events

You might think industry events are a waste of time. If you do, think again. Conferences, seminars, and events can benefit real estate professionals in many ways. First, every industry is constantly changing, and the real estate industry is no exception. It can take a lot of work to keep up with all of the trends and changes occurring on a nearly daily basis. Attending important conferences and events can keep you informed of all the latest developments.

Also, never underestimate the value of networking. In today's very tough job market it is more important than ever before to maintain relationships with others in the industry. Most human resource professionals will tell you that, in the current job market, when a company advertises for a position it is flooded with applications. One of the best ways to stand out from the crowd is networking—knowing someone at the company who can recommend you. Attending industry conferences and events is one of the best ways to meet others in the industry and increase your network.

Key industry conferences are also informative, not just about the latest trends and developments, but about the ways you can improve yourself and your marketability in the industry. Often events provide continuing education and certification courses, one-on-one mentoring and meetings with key leaders in the industry, and ways for you to talk to others about how they are successfully solving the same problems you may be facing. All in all, choosing to attend the right industry events can lead to more opportunities for you down the road.

What follows are some of the conferences and events to consider. Most of the events listed are conferences and conventions of national real estate associations. It is important to keep in mind that many of these national associations have local and state chapters. These local chapters may provide members networking and educational opportunities on a smaller and more affordable scale. Members will also have the opportunity to interact with a strictly local group of professionals, which can lead to job leads and career advancement in your particular geographical area. All in all, checking out both national and local associations and industry events is a great way to learn more about your industry and career path. Some of the major events include:

American Land Title Association Annual Convention This association for abstract and title insurance professionals hosts an annual convention in October each year, reported to be the largest networking event in the industry. Attendees can meet with other professionals, discover the newest industry practices, and take advantage of seminars and other educational opportunities. (http://www.alta.org)

American Planning Association National Conference   City
and community planners can join this association that provides
leadership in the development of vital communities, and attend
its annual national conference each April. More than 5,000
planners attend this conference, which includes symposiums
and workshops geared toward improving communities. Federal
policymakers also speak at the event. (http://www.planning
.org/conference/index.htm)

American Real Estate Society Annual Meeting   This annual
meeting for an association for real estate professionals offers
thoughtful discussion and expert information from executives
and educators in the industry. Topics cover technology, the
economy, and case studies of interest. Attendees can also take
continuing education classes while attending this meeting that
takes place each April. (http://www.aresnet.org/Meetings.phtml)

Appraisal Institute Washington Appraisal Summit   The
Appraisal Institute is a global membership association of
professional real estate appraisers, with more than 25,000
members and 91 chapters throughout the world. It holds
several meetings during the calendar year, and the Washington
Appraisal Summit occurs each July. Advocacy is a big part
of this association's mission, and the Washington Appraisal
summit discusses important legislature and policies affecting
the industry. (http://www.appraisalinstitute.org)

**Building Owners and Managers Association International
Annual Conference**   Members of this association are owners
and managers of commercial properties across the globe. The
annual conference takes place in June, and provides valuable
information for property managers and owners. (http://www
.bomaconvention.org)

**Commercial Real Estate Development Association (NAIOP)
National Forums Symposium**   The leading organization
for developers, owners, and related professionals in office,
industrial, and mixed-use real estate, NAIOP offers an
exclusive conference in August of each year. It is an ideal time
to exchange tips, best practices, and other information with
peers in the industry. (http://www.naiop.org/conferences/
conferences.cfm#2010)

**Commercial Real Estate Women's Network Spring
Leadership Summit & Council Meeting**   Members of this
association for women represent every aspect of the commercial

real estate industry, including law, leasing, brokerage, property management, finance, acquisitions, and engineering. More than 63 percent of the members are CEOs, presidents, owners, partners, or senior managers. The Leadership Summit & Council gives these members an opportunity to share information and tips for career success in this industry. (http://www.crewnetwork.org)

Community Development Society Annual Conference The Community Development Society provides leadership to professionals and citizens in all realms of community development. The annual conference in July includes educational opportunities, speakers, interactive workshops, and presentations from leading professionals. (http://www.comm-dev.org)

Counselors of Real Estate Annual Convention Counselors of Real Estate is a highly selective organization for top real estate advisors. Each October the association has an annual convention. Past topics of discussion include legislative issues, portfolio management, and how to navigate shifting economic markets. (http://www.cre.org/programs_and_events/ac_09_featured_programs.cfm)

Institute of Real Estate Management's iCon The Institute of Real Estate Management (IREM) is has been a source for education, resources, and information for real estate management professionals for more than 75 years. A new event for IREM, iCon is scheduled to occur in October. The organization promises real estate management professionals educational opportunities, seminars, and plenty of networking events and fun. (http://www.irem.org/icon)

Institute of Real Estate Management's Leadership and Legislative Summit Every year in May, IREM members meet in Washington, D.C., to track developments in the real estate management industry. According to the organization, participants in the unique "Leadership and Legislative Summit" have a history of shaping legislation that directly impacts the real estate management industry. (http://www.irem.org/seclins.cfm?sec=conferences&con=2010lls-main.cfm&par=)

Luxury Real Estate Spring Retreat This yearly May retreat caters to real estate professionals who focus on the luxury real estate market. This conference is only for members of the LuxuryRealEstate.com community, the Web site that produces

Who's Who in Luxury Real Estate and *Luxury Real Estate Magazine.* (http://www.luxuryrealestate.com)

National Apartment Association Education Conference and Exposition   This event takes place each June and brings together more than 5,000 multifamily housing professionals for three days of professional development training. The association invites premiere speakers and offers 40 expertly-led education sessions. Three hundred suppliers demonstrate the latest products and services, and networking events help forge new relationships that will advance attendees' careers. (http://www .naahq.org/educonf/Pages/default.aspx)

The National Association of Housing and Redevelopment Officials (NAHRO) National Conference   NAHRO says it is the leading housing and community development advocate for affordable housing and strong, viable communities for all Americans. The association's annual conference provides features a chance to meet with some of the best and brightest experts in the industry. A special focus is on the integration of public, private, and non-profit groups to further the cause of affordable housing. (http://www.nahro.org)

National Association of Mortgage Brokers Legislative and Regulatory Conference   This association for the mortgage broker industry represents the interests of mortgage brokers and homebuyers. Its annual legislative and regulatory conference gives its members the opportunity to hear the latest news and developments of government legislature and policies that affect the industry. (http://www.namb.org/assnfe/ev.asp?ID=114)

National Association of Real Estate Investment Trusts (NAREIT) Investor Forum   NAREIT is the worldwide representative voice for real estate investment trusts and publicly traded real estate companies. Its main focus is in U.S. real estate and capital markets. The forum is an invitation-only retreat for members in good standing that brings together management teams with high-profile plan sponsors, investment managers, advisors, and consultants. (http://www.nareit.com/ meetings/reitweek10)

National Association of Realtors' Conference and Expo   This conference is one of the largest in the industry. It takes place each November and provides attendees with the opportunity to attend workshops, seminars, continuing education classes, and check out the latest real estate-related products and technologies. Attendees can network with professionals from all across the country. (http://www.realtor.org/convention.nsf)

Real Estate Technology Conference and Expo   The goal of this annual March event is to provide tips, information, and resources to real estate professionals who want to take advantage of current and future technology. Much of the conference's program focuses on making the most of Internet marketing, social Web sites, and other current digital marketing methods. (http://www.retechsouth.com)

Virginia Commonwealth University's Real Estate Trends Conference   This annual conference is considered one of the leading forums in the region for the exchange of ideas and information about real estate. The university claims the conference attracts real estate professionals from various industry sectors such as law, finance, construction, development, and brokerage and appraisal, and provides them opportunities to map the future of real estate. (http://www .realestate.vcu.edu/index.htm)

Federal and Local Laws and Regulations

Real estate professionals have a whole bevy of laws and regulations to adhere to. Like any business, there are labor and wage laws, as well as federal, state, and local tax laws. In addition, most professionals must be licensed. Laws that govern whether real estate agents can represent buyers, sellers, or both vary from state to state. Many professionals work in the home construction segment of the industry where there are numerous building laws, codes, and enforcements as well. The real estate professional does not have to know all of them, but a general working knowledge of these codes can be beneficial to those working in this market. Even more labyrinthine are the specific rules and regulations governing the sale of different types of homes. Since short sales and foreclosures are prominent in the industry, agents must be familiar with the laws and policies relating to them. It can be an overwhelming and mind-boggling task to stay on top of all things legal in the real estate industry. While the information below is a good start, it is not intended to replace your own thorough investigation of the specific laws and regulations you need to follow in your business and location.

Affordable Housing Preservation Exit Tax

Many real estate agents and brokers believe that the current tax system makes it unnecessarily difficult to maintain government-financed or government-supported affordable housing projects. The primary obstacle, they say, are "exit taxes"—taxes paid on the recapture of depreciation and other deductions, accrued when selling a property. According to the Local Initiatives Support Coalition (LISC), a community development organization, "In some affordable housing transactions, sellers may face a significant exit tax even when they do not receive net cash at sale." These taxes act as a deterrent for owners of government-financed or government-assisted properties to continue operating them as affordable housing. As the National Association of Home Builders (NAHB) says, "Sellers are put into a position that they must pay the tax out of other assets. This situation acts as an effective prohibition on the sales of affordable properties that can have an adverse effect on needed rehabilitations of the housing."

The LISC, NAHB, and other organizations believe that owners as well as property managers are entitled to access to adequate capital for maintenance of their rental housing, no matter what kind of tenant their property secures. Real estate agents and brokers are likewise committed to preserving and/or increasing affordable housing so as to increase the pool of available renters. Suggestions to reform the exit tax code include legislation to make permanent the reduction in ordinary long term capital gains taxes, as well as legislation that provides exit tax relief on affordable properties. If such changes are enacted, owners would be able to easily recapitalize and renovate their properties.

Affordable Housing Tax Credit

Another issue real estate agents are looking for the government to correct is a lack of federal tax incentives to help lower-income individuals and families purchase affordable housing. In 2002, President George W. Bush proposed a single-family tax credit to promote the building and development of affordable housing in urban centers. For this plan, developers and investors would be given tax credits to construct or rehabilitate housing for buyers with an annual income of 80 percent or less of the area median income (AMI) of a given region. While this plan had the support of over 40 industry organizations that cited it as a means of increasing the supply of entry-level housing in often overlooked areas, many low-income housing advocates believed the policy favored developers and that the qualifying income level was too high to help those most in need. Additionally, the substantial cost of the proposal ($16 billion over 10 years) consistently caused it to stall out long before it had a chance to become legislation. Many of the bill's supporters have since identified several ways to reduce the cost without undermining the utility of the credit. To date, however, no affordable housing tax credit proposal has emerged from these discussions.

Appraisal Mortgage Fraud

Many real estate experts and educators feel that appraisal fraud may have been another factor leading to the mortgage crisis. In a survey by October Research, close to 90 percent of appraisers reported that mortgage loan originators used improper influence by asking them to make a specific appraisal value. Because referrals and repeat business are vital to the welfare of appraisers' business, 70 percent of the appraisers surveyed said they feared harm to their business if they did not comply with these requests.

For obvious reasons, various professional appraiser organizations and licensing boards as well as a wide variety of realtor associations stand in strong opposition to such practices. Besides the ethical concerns, the overstating or undervaluing of a particular piece of real estate harms consumers by distorting the lending process. In attempts to combat the trend to "tweak" the numbers of an appraisal, a series of regulations known as the Home Valuation Code of Conduct (HVCC) was introduced in March of 2008. This joint agreement between Freddie Mac, the Federal Housing Finance Agency (FHFA), and the New York State Attorney General seeks "to curb the banking industry's pressure on independent appraisers to produce appraisal reports that met their lending needs instead of reflecting the true market value of the properties being appraised," according to the industry insider Web site Appraisalscoop.com. Despite these efforts, however, appraisal fraud continues to be a problem. Studies by the Mortgage Asset Research Institute (MARI) as reported by the *Washington Post* show that appraisal fraud increased by 50 percent in 2009 and is currently the fastest-growing fraudulent enterprise in the real estate system. While no single solution to such a widespread

INTERVIEW

The Need for Service

Barry Salotollo
Owner, Westchester Spaces, New York, New York

What are some general tips for succeeding in real estate?
Real estate is a career, not a job. You need to become the best at what you do. That is a cliché, but it means a lot. Study your craft after you get the license—that is where the real education begins. Make sure you know more than your customers. There is a lot of information out there on the Internet and beyond, so you really have to be on top of your game. And remember, you will not get rich quick—you have to do the work. One more thing: If the customer does not like the place you are showing them, no matter how good you are at schmoozing, you are not selling it. Move on.

What are some current developments in the field of real estate?
We are moving into the 21st century in terms of marketing and technology, so people are using the Internet more. We have kind of captured the online market here, so it is an exciting time. Technology will make us even stronger when the industry comes back. Setting up systems with computers and marketing will make the situation less problematic for us.

problem exists, industry professionals stress the need for due diligence when drafting loans, as well as a concerted effort by banks to hire vetted, ethical appraisers.

Banks in Real Estate

In early 2001, the Federal Reserve Board and the U.S. Treasury Department proposed rules to expand the powers of national bank conglomerates by allowing them to engage in real estate brokerage and management then reclassify these activities as financial in nature. Seeking to preserve the autonomy of their field, most professional real estate organizations opposed these changes. Realtors feared that if banks were allowed to engage in real estate brokerage,

What challenges should someone entering the real estate industry expect in this day and age?

There are a lot of issues, depending on one's area. New York City, Westchester, and high-end sections of Brooklyn are by the water. Prices are set by builders and mortgage people who appraise the properties. Prices, despite the economy, are still high around here. [Normal middle-class people] simply cannot get a place in Manhattan, even with the drops in prices. Recession or no, Manhattan is the place to be, and it is priced accordingly, even with prices down 15 to 20 percent. Prices still run $1,500 to $1,600 dollars a square foot, even with price reductions—and people are paying it. The high demand leads to overvalued property. Also, people have been leveraging property, investing and borrowing against it. This makes equity skyrocket, which leads some people to refinance on top of it. What happens is when values go down, people find themselves owing more than their property is worth. Add downsizing and job losses, and people get overwhelmed.

What industry trends can we expect to see in the coming years?

We are seeing an uptick in new constructions, sales, and pricing a little, but we are a year or so off until we level and then head back upward. Right now, I focus on analysis in the day-to-day. It is the wave of the future—small companies and "mom-and-pop" offices that do not embrace the Internet will be missing out over the next five to 10 years. Our goal is to make sure we know more than our customers so we can be on the top of our game. We are stressing networking, personality, and ethics. Servicing customers is number one, and repeat referrals are key. That is what I am seeing.

it would create an unfair competitive environment, since banks would have direct access to cheap sources of capital. They also feared that it would result in compromised lending decisions and conflicts of interest. Citing historical precedent, the National Association of Realtors argued that the Bank Holding Company Act of 1956 and the Gramm-Leach-Bliley Act of 1999 do not authorize banking firms to provide real estate brokerage and property management services. In response to these grievances, the government stepped in and permanently blocked the Federal and Treasury Department from expanding bank authority: On March 11, 2009, President Obama signed into law the FY2009 Omnibus Appropriations Act, which permanently prohibits banks from entering the real estate brokerage and management businesses.

On the Cutting Edge

Videos

When it comes to hot technology, one of the latest trends hitting the Internet waves is the use of videos on real estate companies' Web sites. Embedding videos that market new home listings, or even explain the latest trends in that market are sure ways to capture new business. Today, consumers are more educated, and they are used to getting instant information. Videos provide the information in a way that also sells the company.

To make the most of your video, make sure the on-camera talent is friendly, can speak knowledgeably, and the pace is not too slow. You will lose people quickly if your introduction takes up most of the video. Also, keep videos short, if possible. Unless the video is mainly of new listings, it should be five minutes or less.

Down-Payment Assistance

In recent years, sellers wishing to sell their homes to particular buyers have volunteered to assist the buyers with their down payments. Those in the industry say that this practice raises the price of a home. It also leads to improper underwriting, appraisals, and eventually a greater likelihood of default and foreclosure. In 2006, the IRS published a notice that it would remove the 501(c)(3) (non-profit) designation from entities where the primary function was to funnel down payment money from sellers to buyers to assist in a home buying transaction. This affects the Federal Housing Authority, since it allows down payment assistance from a 501(c)(3) entity. Following this new rule, seller-financed down payment through nonprofits is now ineligible for use by FHA borrowers.

The Fair Housing Act

Formally known as the Civil Rights Act of 1968 and amended in 1988, the Fair Housing Act prohibits discrimination in the sale, rental, and financing of all residences based on race, national origin, religion, sex, familial status, and disability. As of 2010, 20 state and numerous local laws additionally prohibit discrimination on the basis of sexual orientation. The Department of Housing and Urban Development has proposed prohibiting discrimination based on sexual orientation in all HUD-funded housing, and though the proposal has yet to become law, many in the industry are in support of it.

The Fair Housing Act affects the real estate industry in various ways. Property owners and building managers must alter their policies, for instance, to allow people with disabilities equal housing opportunities. A common example is that a landlord who does not allow pets in his or her building may have to make an exception for a visually impaired tenant with a guide dog. Realtors and mortgage lenders must beware of "redlining" tactics, a term that originates with the New Deal practice of outlining low-income neighborhoods in red on maps to designate their undesirability for investment. These maps were then circulated to lenders and developers to guide the flow of capital away from inner cities and into suburban areas. While the Fair Housing Act took steps to curb this practice, the fact remains that it is still a major problem in the industry. Finally, those on the construction and rehabilitation end of the housing market must be aware that their work—particularly large projects in urban centers—will be scrutinized by research institutions and other watchdog groups. Common offenses include substandard construction, poor environmental conditions (including mold, asbestos, and water damage), and failure to comply with current safety codes.

Commercial Real Estate Lending

It is clear from industry research conducted by the National Association of Realtors and other organizations that the commercial real estate market is still in the midst of a serious financial crisis. Studies show that nearly $150 billion of commercial real estate debt will mature in 2010 with another $500 billion maturing in the following three years. Many of the properties tied to these loans have debt that exceeds the current value of the property, and owners will face serious trouble when attempting to refinance them. Analysts expect that this may well prove detrimental to the U.S. economic recovery, as the commercial real estate industry is a $6.7 trillion sector of the nation's economy. By the end of 2012, it is estimated that some $153 billion in commercial mortgage loans will come due, and it is expected that close to $100 billion of that will face difficulty being refinanced. Though there is no clear way to resolve this widespread issue facing the commercial market, suggestions have been made to form mortgage insurance programs to protect performing commercial loans; to make loan term extensions available from the Federal Reserve; and to improve lending access for small businesses, thus leading to smaller-scale and more manageable investments.

Future Outlook

The experts will tell you: The real estate market will improve, and in fact, *is* improving. According to the July 2009 quarterly report from Prudential Real Estate Investors, the nation's economic turnaround is underway. According to the report, many economic indicators are showing signs of new life, which should mean good news for the residential real estate market. The commercial market generally tends to move more slowly than home sales do, and it depends upon a healthy employment picture. In light of news that though job losses have slowed and unemployment is still rising (just not as much), PREI does not see much improvement for job growth until sometime in 2010. The report warns that the commercial sector "will continue to deteriorate" until then.

The report also warns that the process of deleveraging commercial properties (that is, reducing the amount of debt one owes on a property) has begun and will take years to complete. In the meantime, loan defaults are on the rise, which may make lenders reluctant to "support a robust level of new transactions or refinancings. The government's efforts may get the commercial mortgage-backed securities market restarted this summer, but deal activity will be limited at first." The report does not inspire confidence in property values either, as they continue to spiral downward. According to the document, values have dropped nearly 25 percent since their last peak in the first quarter of 2008, and PREI expects them to fall at least another 15 percent before rebounding. The report continues to forecast a difficult time for investors and owners until jobs recover, particularly in commercial real estate.

This industry, by nature, runs in cycles. As we have seen throughout history, periods of prosperity turn into times of crisis and back again. Right now, the U.S. real estate market is slowly pulling itself out of a huge mess. It took years to create this situation; it will take some time before we see a big upswing. Think about it: this nation survived the Great Depression, world wars, bank scandals, gas crises, and recessions. Every time, the market corrects itself and eventually works its way back to a point where it can again flourish.

Happy days will be here again for our real estate industry, and probably before 2010 comes to a close. This forthcoming wave of success will come to pass because of the drive, persistence, patience, and knowledge of talented, dedicated real estate professionals old and new who refused to give in to negativity. Clearly, this is not a pursuit for the timid. But if you have taken to heart the reality of the market and the challenges you could face and still marvel at the possibilities of a real estate career, there is no doubt you will be welcomed into the industry with open arms.

Chapter 3

On the Job

Most people are attracted to the real estate industry for two reasons: they enjoy working with people, and they relish the flexible work schedule that being a real estate agent can provide. Whether you wish to be a residential agent, commercial agent, appraiser, or work in a corporate environment, there is a place for you in the industry. As one of the nation's largest employers you can almost take your pick of location or branch of the industry. If being an agent is not your first choice of career, there are many other jobs within the real estate industry, such as marketing professionals and accounting and tax experts. There are even jobs for those who prefer to be hands-on. The industry is always in need of energetic people with fresh ideas and dedication.

Below you will find an A through Z listing, broken up by industry segment, of the jobs available in the industry today. Each listing will describe the job, education or certification needed, whether there are any direct reports associated with the job, and the associated career path. That way you can easily chart your path to your end career result.

Administrative and Professional

In both the residential and commercial real estate sectors, these are the jobs that move the machinery of the industry.

Accountant

Accounting is an important function for any operation, large or small. Often accounts tie in to inventory, human resource management, and other measurements of operational efficiency. Small brokerages may hire accounting firms to manage this function or do the basics themselves. Large brokerages, corporations, commercial real estate companies, and real estate investment trusts may employ in-house accountants or CPAs to ensure accounting is accurate, meets federal, state, and local regulations, and is providing the reporting necessary for management to make ongoing decisions.

The real estate accountant will review property management financial reports and write monthly, quarterly, and annual reports for the company and potentially for some clients. Most accounting positions require a college education, and most states require 30 hours of additional college coursework beyond the four-year degree program. Some may require a certified public accountant (CPA) designation. Experience as an accountant or CPA in the real estate industry is usually required or considered a plus. As one moves through the ranks, supervisory and managerial positions are often available. In large operations this career path could lead to executive positions, such as controller and chief financial officer.

Administrative Assistant

Administrative assistants perform an important function at most real estate companies. They can be the first contact potential buyers or sellers have with the agency, and so need to be professional, friendly, and customer service-oriented. Administrative assistants perform various administrative functions, from preparing mailings and answering phones to preparing contracts or legal forms used in property sales. Administrative assistants also process, file, and deliver information clients and staff members need. No secondary education (college level or higher) is usually required, although some real estate agencies may prefer assistants with previous experience in real estate, or with some college or business coursework. Depending on the size and type of the organization, administrative assistants could be promoted to senior assistant, executive assistant, or office manager. If the administrative assistant decides he or she enjoys the real estate industry, he or she could become an agent.

Apartment Manager

Apartment managers are hired by the apartment owner or company to handle the day-to-day business of a specific apartment complex. Depending on the size of the complex, apartment managers may be responsible for negotiating leases, completing and processing all lease applications, contracting with service providers, and ensuring that the property is being maintained according to company standards. At larger complexes, the apartment manager may be responsible for supervising a team of leasing consultants. Some smaller complexes may expect the apartment manager to clean common areas such as stairways and hallways.

Apartment managers are not required to have a college degree, but they do need to have a high school diploma or GED. Most complexes require apartment managers to have several months to a year of previous apartment managing experience. Apartment managers need to have good communication and organizational skills, as well as strong people skills. Apartment managers can become certified property managers through professional real estate organizations such as Institute of Real Estate Management (http://www.irem.org) or the National Association of Realtors (http://www.realtor.org). In large operations there is plenty of room for growth for the apartment manager. Certified property managers can be promoted to business manager or district or regional manager of companies with several properties.

Property Manager/Assistant Property Manager

The property and assistant property manager are concerned with the day-to-day operations of investment properties, whether they are apartments, office buildings, industrial complexes, or shopping malls. The property manager must ensure that each building is meeting its income goals and is being maintained. Assistant property managers work with property managers of more than one building, to assist with all of the administrative work that goes along with the job. These managers contract with service providers and negotiate rental contracts.

A college degree along with three to four years of experience is usually required for property managers and/or their assistants, although assistant managers may have less experience. Property and assistant property managers need to have good business, organizational, and time management skills, and be able to skillfully negotiate with potential renters and contractors. Certifications can be obtained through professional real estate organizations such as Institute of Real Estate Management or the National Association of Realtors. The successful property manager, especially one who is certified, can be promoted to higher-level positions, managing larger facilities or a larger number of facilities. Property managers can also earn upper management positions within large real estate management firms.

Commercial Real Estate Broker

Commercial real estate brokers represent potential buyers, renters, or sellers of commercial properties, whether they are manufacturing facilities, office buildings, or retail buildings such as malls or strip malls. They may also work with investors who wish to acquire a property for income purposes. Commercial real estate brokers analyze various aspects of properties, from their values to future income potential, in order to create purchase or lease arrangements acceptable to both parties. They may also assist clients with financing arrangements.

Commercial real estate brokers need to possess a bachelor's degree and three to five years of real estate experience. They need to have strong organizational, negotiating, and analytical skills, and must be licensed in the state in which they work. Each state's licensing requirements may vary, so check with your state to determine yours. Professional licensing is available through the CCIM Institute (http://www.ccim.com). Depending on the size of the organization, a commercial real estate broker could be promoted to the broker in charge, or he or she could decide to start his or her own brokerage.

Construction Estimator

The construction estimator usually works for a general construction company. It is the estimator's job to determine the costs involved in a large construction project. He or she typically conducts a site visit to determine the needs for electricity, water, and other utilities. The estimator also develops a list of all materials needed to complete the project and reviews any subcontractors' bids. The estimator of a large company will turn in his or her report to the chief estimator, who will finalize the company's bid for the project. An inaccurate estimate can severely affect the profitability of the project.

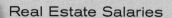

Real Estate Salaries

Below are the annual salaries of real estate agents and brokers in the real estate industry as of May 2008, according to the U.S. Bureau of Labor Statistics. The median annual wages, including commissions, of salaried real estate sales agents were $40,150. The middle 50 percent earned between $27,390 and $64,820. The bottom 10 percent earned less than $21,120, and the highest 10 percent earned more than $101,860. Median annual wages in the industries employing the largest number of real estate sales agents were:

Residential building construction	$49,620
Land subdivision	44,410
Offices of real estate agents and brokers	41,320
Activities related to real estate	36,410
Lessors of real estate	32,150

Median annual wages, including commissions, of salaried real estate brokers were $57,500. The middle 50 percent earned between $36,420 and $93,970. Median annual wages in the industries employing the largest number of real estate brokers were:

Residential building construction	$63,280
Offices of real estate agents and brokers	59,710
Activities related to credit intermediation	57,740
Activities related to real estate	56,140
Lessors of real estate	47,230

A bachelor's degree and up to two years of experience in real estate development or construction are required to obtain an estimator position. Estimators must also have the ability to read blueprints and interpret construction drawings, and have strong analytical, problem-solving, and project management skills. Estimators can receive certification through two organizations: the Association for the Advancement of Cost Engineering International (http://www

.aacei.org), or the Society of Cost Estimating and Analysis (http://www.sceaonline.net).

Estimators have a few career paths open to them. Some can be promoted within a company to senior estimator or chief estimator. Some estimators may obtain these more advanced positions at other companies. Estimators have also become project managers in construction or at industrial engineering departments of manufacturers. They can also become consultants, or operate their own estimating business.

Construction Project Manager

Construction project managers oversee a construction project from start to finish. As early as the design phase, the construction project manager begins work, scheduling and coordinating all construction work that must take place, including hiring and managing construction crews, subcontractors, and other site workers. The construction project manager is responsible for ensuring that the construction project is completed on time and within budget. Project managers may work for construction firms, construction management firms, real estate development firms, or may act as self-employed consultants.

College degrees in construction management, engineering, architecture, or a related field are usually required. Project managers must possess strong organizational and problem-solving skills, as well as an eye for detail. Professional certifications are available, primarily through two professional associations: the American Institute of Contractors (http://www.americancontractorsinstitute.com), or the Construction Management Association of America (http://www.cmaanet.org). Highly successful project managers have many advancement options open to them. Some become promoted to senior project management or supervisory positions within their company or organization. Others may obtain these advanced positions or even executive roles at other organizations. Some project managers may choose to become self-employed consultants.

Development Manager

The development manager is a master of multi-tasking. He or she must be creative, but also a detail-minded analyzer, knowledgeable about many facets of real estate and development. The development manager will acquire a site or empty building and develop it, sometimes repurposing it. For example, he or she may purchase an abandoned factory and convert it into luxury condominiums. He or she will then need to get regulatory and zoning approval changes, if needed, as well as line up a number of tenants and obtain financing. He or she must also have extensive knowledge of construction processes and ensure that the project is completed on time and within budget. Development managers work with architects, engineers, and leasing teams to bring a project to fruition. They may work for real estate development companies or as a self-employed business owner.

Development managers are required to hold a bachelor's degree in architecture, business, or engineering. Most real estate developers will expect development managers to have a minimum of three to five years of experience in real estate marketing, sales, or building management. Development managers should have excellent communication, problem-solving, and negotiating skills. They should also have a great deal of knowledge of construction. There are no certifications associated with these positions.

Development managers may be promoted by earning larger and more complicated projects within their company. Successful development managers may also earn promotions into management positions within the real estate development firm, or be offered partnerships.

Executive Management

Executive level personnel are expected to lead an organization and ensure it meets measurable objectives. They are considered the visionaries that take a company to new levels of success. They must also be able to communicate effectively, and inspire others in the organization to excel. Executives in real estate should be able to provide leadership and decision-making skills based on extensive knowledge and experience in the industry. Executives are expected to have advanced degrees in business, architecture, engineering, construction management, or other related fields. They should also have several years of demonstrated success as a leader in the industry.

Information Technology (IT) Professional

IT professionals can find many opportunities in the real estate industry. Since so much of a real estate professional's work is completed with the use of a computer and related technology, there is a growing demand for IT professionals in this field. IT professionals may write computer programs to meet company needs, maintain computers and networks, phone equipment, and Internet and intranet networks. They may also design or manage programs for completing required real estate and governmental documentation. A college degree plus appropriate software and network certifications may be required depending on the specific job. Employers also prefer professionals with some on the job experience. In addition to technical skills, IT professionals may need to possess excellent communication, organizational, and project management skills. IT departments offer promotions in the form of managerial positions. Very large companies often designate an executive position for IT, called chief technology officer.

Leasing Agent

Leasing agents are hired by landlords to keep their buildings occupied by tenants, whether the building is comprised of offices or retail businesses. The leasing agent must have a good understanding of the location of the building and the surrounding community in order to know what kinds of businesses are most likely to want the space and succeed in the building. Tenants may want to know if there is a large labor pool or the demographics of the local residents. Leasing agents will work with the tenant or his or her agent to negotiate the terms of the contract and space. Some tenants may have special needs that must be met. Once terms are agreed, the agent then writes the contract and makes sure tenant and the landlord both sign it.

Leasing agents must have a bachelor's degree in business administration or a related field. Most landlords look for leasing agents with at least two to five years of experience in real estate or sales. Leasing agents should also have effective communication skills, as well as organizational and negotiating skills. There are no certifications associated with this position, however some states require licensing. To determine whether you need a real estate license to be a leasing agent in your state, check with your state's licensing board.

Leasing agents may be appointed to more senior positions within the real estate management company, becoming leasing managers or directors. Some leasing agents can earn more money and prestige by becoming consultants employed by accounting firms or real estate consulting firms.

Maintenance Supervisor

The maintenance supervisor at an apartment complex or other facility is in charge of maintaining all of the facility's buildings, equipment, and grounds. He or she usually has a staff of groundskeepers who perform the duties he or she assigns to keep the buildings and grounds looking their best. The maintenance supervisor may hire, train, schedule, and evaluate all of his or her employees. He or she may also be required to carry a pager and respond to after-hours maintenance emergencies.

A maintenance supervisor must have a high school diploma. A college education is not necessary, but most facilities prefer to hire supervisors that have at least three to five years of property maintenance experience. Additionally, a maintenance supervisor should have good leadership skills since he or she will be supervising others. He or she should also have strong organizational and communication skills. Successful maintenance supervisors could be promoted to assistant property manager, and eventually property manager of the facility they supervise. If the property owner has more than one facility, a supervisor could also be promoted to a larger facility with additional staff members.

Marketing Representative/Supervisor/Director

Marketing department personnel are responsible for successfully marketing a business, whether the business is a residential or commercial real estate firm, apartment complex, construction firm, or development company. Marketing campaigns must meet budget requirements. Personnel will develop marketing material and choose appropriate advertising and promotional outlets. A college degree in business with an emphasis on marketing is required. Higher level positions may require an MBA degree. Certifications are not required to obtain employment, but are available through the American Marketing Association (http://www.mar ketingpower.com). Lower level positions may require some previous industry experience, at least one to two years. Higher level positions may require advertising agency experience or extensive knowledge of marketing strategies, techniques, and channels. A typical marketing professional begins as a marketing coordinator or representative then advances to marketing supervisor. A supervisor can be promoted to marketing director. Depending on the size of the organization, executive level positions may be the final step in a real estate marketing career. The very successful marketer may choose to start his or her own marketing firm specializing in the real estate industry.

Portfolio Manager

Portfolio managers may be hired by real estate development companies, real estate management companies, and consulting firms. They may focus on one particular development project for a client, or several properties. When managing a single development the portfolio manager represents the client's interests and works with architects, engineers, and construction managers to resolve property issues. The portfolio manager does not get involved in day-to-day operations, but focuses more on the "big picture." Portfolio managers who oversee several properties analyze the values of the properties, including their income, costs, and resale potential. The portfolio manager will keep close watch on changing markets and advise the client when it may be an optimum time to sell or buy a property.

Portfolio managers must have at least a bachelor's degree in business management or related field. Employers also look for portfolio managers who have at least three years of experience in commercial management or property development. Portfolio managers should have excellent research and analytical skills. They must know how to monitor real estate markets and communities, analyze and create spreadsheets, and determine the value of properties. They should also have excellent communication and organizational skills. In some states the portfolio manager may be required to hold a real estate license. Professional certifications are available through the Building Owners and Managers Institute (http://www.bomi.org), the Institute of Real Estate Management (http://www.irem.org), the CCIM Institute (http://www.ccim.com), and CoreNet Global (http://www.corenetglobal.org).

At large companies, the portfolio manager could be promoted to manage larger, more complicated portfolios, or become a supervisor of other portfolio managers. Some real estate management firms have directors of real estate. Successful portfolio managers usually fill these positions.

Real Estate Advisor

The real estate advisor is an expert that investors of all kinds go to when developing a property or portfolio of properties. Different than a real estate broker, the real estate advisor is an independent real estate expert with no financial interest involved in his or her opinion. Most real estate advisors work for development companies, financial and business consulting firms, and real estate consulting companies. The real estate advisor determines the value of properties and their potential income, as well as projected value, in order to advise the client of the investment value of the property. Often a real estate advisor is hired to determine whether a property the client is interested in purchasing is a good investment. Real estate advisors may perform site inspections, development assistance, and review deals, among other functions.

Real estate advisors must have a bachelor's degree in business, economics, or related field. Some firms may require the advisor to hold a master's degree. A real estate advisor should also possess three to five years of experience in real estate financial analysis and related duties. He or she should have very strong analytical skills, excellent communication skills, and research skills. In some states the real estate advisor will need to obtain a real estate license. Real estate advisors can earn certifications through the CCIM Institute (http://www.ccim.com), the Society of Industrial and Office Realtors (http://www.sior.com), and the Counselors of Real Estate (http://www.cre.org). The typical career path for real estate advisors is a promotion to senior advisor or research director of a large consulting firm. The real estate advisor may have more success obtaining these promotions if he or she earns a master's degree.

Real Estate Attorney

The real estate attorney handles all legal matters relating to real estate, from investigating zoning issues and real estate transactions to representing clients in real estate legal disputes to interpreting local real estate laws. Most real estate attorneys work for a firm that offers a variety of legal services for clients, although some work for business consulting firms. In addition to a law degree, potential real estate lawyers must pass a state bar examination to be licensed to practice law. Most states also require applicants to pass a separate written ethics examination. Continuing education is required.

Best Practice

Choosing the Right Real Estate Job for You

How do you know what job in the real estate industry will work for you? Unfortunately, no career comes with a guarantee. In the real estate industry, there are two primary types of jobs, those that are sales related, and those that are not. If you like the idea of selling real estate or being part of real estate sales, you have narrowed down your choices somewhat. You can sell residential real estate or commercial. When it comes to non-sales positions you have more to choose from: whether you want to do inspections, process loans, or work in an administrative capacity. Once you have narrowed down your choices, talk to others who are doing the job now and shadow them if that is possible. There are also several books you can read and Web sites you can visit that have quizzes to evaluate your skills and interests. After taking them, they will recommend some career choices best suited to your interests and abilities. Examples are *Career Tests: 25 Revealing Self-Tests to Help You Find and Succeed at the Perfect Career* by Louis H. Janda, Free-Career-Test.com, and LiveCareer.com.

Attorneys need to be detail oriented, analytical, and thorough. They must work well with people, have excellent communication and people skills, and should inspire trust and confidence in their clients. Depending on the size of the firm, attorneys may become managers or achieve the status of partner or senior partner of a firm. Successful attorneys may also choose to launch their own law firms.

Risk Manager

Risk managers evaluate a property's risks and design and implement programs to reduce them. Risk managers must prepare for "worst case scenarios" such as natural disasters and terrorist attacks, and have recovery plans in place. Risk managers also look at a property's facilities to determine of there are too many risks to safety and profitability. For example, if an apartment complex is in a high-crime neighborhood the risk manager may recommend extensive fencing around the property or other increased security measures. The risk manager may also evaluate the entire business's risk and make appropriate recommendations. In the real estate industry, risk managers may work at real estate development and consulting firms as well as property management companies.

Risk managers will need to have a bachelor's degree in accounting, finance, or a related field. Some employers prefer managers with a master's degree or MBA. Most risk managers should have somewhere between five and 10 years of experience in real estate under their belt. The most important skills risk managers should possess are strong analytical skills and organizational and communication skills. There are certifications for some types of risk managers, especially those working within the financial industry, although there is not a certification specifically for real estate risk management. Depending on the size of the company and risk management department, management and executive opportunities may exist.

Tax Manager

Tax managers are usually accountants that specialize in tax laws and accounting. They are primarily employed by large real estate firms, real estate development firms, and real estate management companies with ongoing tax and accounting needs. Tax specialists will assure that all financial aspects of the company are properly reported on the business tax returns and have extensive knowledge of tax laws so that the company is taking full advantage of all deductions.

Most tax positions require at least a bachelor's degree in accounting or a related field. If a tax specialist is required to file a report with the Securities and Exchange Commission (SEC), he or she is required by law to be a certified public accountant (CPA). CPAs are licensed by their State Board of Accountancy. The Accreditation Council for Accountancy and Taxation, a satellite organization of the National Society of Accountants, confers four designations on accountants who specialize in tax accounting: Accredited Business Accountant (ABA), Accredited Tax Advisor (ATA), Accredited Tax Preparer (ATP), and Elder Care Specialist (ECS). Candidates for the ABA must pass an exam. Candidates for the other designations must complete the required coursework and in some cases also pass an exam. Tax specialists also need to have excellent math and analytical skills. Depending on the size of the company and the accounting and tax department, supervisory, management, and executive level positions may be available.

Residential Real Estate

The following professionals are responsible for guiding people through what may be the most important investment of their lives— a home.

New Home Sales Representative

The new home sales representative's goal is to sell new homes in a new housing development. The representative gathers sales leads through Web sites, trade shows, direct mail marketing, and word of mouth. The representative then contacts each lead to determine whether they qualify to buy a home. Once the lead becomes a buyer the representative helps the buyer obtain a mortgage and serves as their liaison until the sale is closed. The representative must keep a close eye on the housing market and competitors' sales. He or she may also collect sales data and create sales reports for developers.

New home sales representatives are only required to have a high school diploma, although some developers prefer candidates who have completed some college coursework. Developers also look for representatives with one to two years of successful sales experience. Representatives should have the ability to generate sales leads and have excellent communication, problem-solving, and computer skills. Certification can be obtained through the National Association of Home Builders (http://www.nahb.org). Successful representatives can become sales managers for their developments. If the developers have more than one development, there may also be regional manager positions. Executive sales positions are available at larger development companies.

Real Estate Buyer's Agent

Real estate home buyer's agents specialize in finding the right home for their client, a home buyer. Real estate laws vary from state to state and some states do not permit this kind of representation. For those that do, the buyer's agent works for a real estate firm that does not take any listings. In other words, they exclusively represent buyers rather than sellers. The real estate buyer's agent meets with the buyers to determine their housing needs, and then finds homes for sale in the neighborhoods and price ranges they have requested. After visiting different homes, the hope is that the buyer will find one he or she likes and put in an offer to buy it. The real estate buyer's agent negotiates the sales contract terms and helps the buyer obtain financing.

The real estate buyer's agent needs to have a high school diploma. Some brokerages may also require their agents to have college degrees. Buyer's agents should have adequate knowledge of the residential real estate market. He or she should also have very strong people and sales skills, good organizational and communication skills, and knowledge of basic computer programs and proficiency with Internet research. All real estate buyer's agents are required to obtain real estate sales licenses.

The career path of the buyer's agent depends on the size of the brokerage and the goals of the agent. If the agent works for a large brokerage, he or she could become the office manager or agent in charge. Or the buyer's agent could choose to start his or her own brokerage. The agent would first need to obtain a state broker's license. Other career options for the buyer's agent include becoming property managers or mortgage loan originators.

Residential Real Estate Broker

The residential real estate broker is different than an agent in one important way: he or she has a state broker's license. Most real estate agents do not have a broker's license. They work as sales agents for the broker and earn commission. Typically their expenses are deducted from their commissions. The real estate broker represents either buyers or sellers; in some states, he or she can represent both. For sellers the broker works to sell the property for the most money, and for the buyer he or she works to negotiate the lowest sales price. Additionally the broker may assist the buyer in obtaining financing, preparing the sales contract, and providing housing market consultations.

Brokers are usually not required to possess a college degree. However, some clients prefer a degreed candidate. Past sales experience can also increase a broker's chances for success. The real estate broker needs to possess high quality sales and negotiating skills, as well as excellent communication and organizational skills. Certifications are not offered, though professional designations can be obtained through the National Association of Realtors.

Residential Sales Assistant

Residential sales assistants are most often hired by larger residential brokerages. Sales assistants provide administrative and other assistance to sales agents and brokers. Their duties vary from brokerage to brokerage, but most will answer phones, schedule home visits, collect information for sales transactions, deliver documents to those who need them, and assist sales agents with problem-solving and routine office functions.

Employers generally look for sales assistants who have a high school diploma or GED and a few years of sales experience. Sales assistants should have good phone and interpersonal communication skills, organizational skills, and the ability to take direction. Sales assistants should also have working knowledge of computer office programs. In most brokerages, the sales assistant position is considered an apprenticeship toward becoming a full-time sales agent or broker. Usually within a year sales assistants are expected to earn their real estate licenses and begin working as sales agents. In large brokerages, a sales assistant may choose to become the office supervisor or manager.

Real Estate-Related Positions

While not explicitly involved with construction or client-to-seller relations, these positions are nevertheless crucial to the well-being of the industry.

Appraiser (Residential and Commercial)

Both residential and commercial appraisers work for banks, insurance companies, or appraisal firms. An appraisal determines the value and particular designation (i.e., residential, commercial, or mixed-use) of a property. Appraisals are usually required for mortgages or other financing, as the bank must know how much a property is worth in order to use it as collateral. An appraiser visits a property to see the state it is in, as well as the condition of the surrounding neighborhood. He or she then looks at the values of similar properties in the same area. From this information an appraisal is made.

Appraisers are required to hold a bachelor's degree. Appraisers must also earn a state license and become certified through the successful completion of a number of exams. Most employers want the appraiser to have at least a year of prior experience in real estate assessment. Since appraisers work independently and primarily with data, they need to have strong analytical skills, and good computer and organizational skills. Depending on the size and type of the business the appraiser works for, he or she could become a supervisor or manager or an appraiser reviewer, verifying all of the appraisals completed before they are submitted. Supervisors or managers will also oversee other appraisers and schedule their work. Appraisers who advance to the top of the field and earn the highest appraiser designation can choose to launch their own appraisal firms.

Architect

Architects design and develop plans for the construction of new buildings or the remodeling of existing ones. Architects must work closely with clients, listening to all of their needs and then providing a plan that will meet them as closely as possible within budget constraints. Architects design all kinds of buildings—churches, homes, offices, schools, manufacturing facilities, and apartment complexes, to name a few—and must understand the various building code requirements of each. Architects earn a five-year degree and must

Professional
Ethics

Representing Both Buyer and Seller

It is not uncommon for a real estate sales agent to end up representing both the buyer and the seller of a property. In most states this is legal. However, it is a tricky place for the agent to be. In most states, if the agent contracted with the seller, his or her ultimate responsibility is to the seller. This needs to be communicated to the buyer before the buyer agrees to become your client. The best ethical way to handle this situation is to be clear in all communication about what your duties and responsibilities are to all involved, prior to them agreeing to the situation.

apprentice for a number of years, typically three, before working on their own. In addition, they must be licensed through the state. Architects should have very strong creative skills, as well as the ability to translate ideas into a workable design. Continuing education classes are a must if they are to maintain their licenses.

Assessor

Assessors determine the value of a property for municipal tax purposed. They are hired by the city or county to keep property values current, advise owners of their taxes, and maintain all property value information records. Assessors may be required to do site inspections of certain properties. They use very similar methods as appraisers to determine the value of the property. Assessors will need to hold a bachelor's degree in real estate or related field. Years of experience required by the city or county will vary, but typically averages anywhere between one and three years. Most states require that assessors be licensed. Check with your state licensing agency for requirements.

Commercial Loan Underwriter

A commercial loan underwriter receives commercial loan application packages and analyzes them to determine whether they should be approved. Underwriters are looking at two primary aspects of the package: the financial fitness of the business to pay the loan off, and whether the property under consideration could be resold for enough to pay back the loan should the borrower default. Underwriters will also ensure that the package and documentation meets all bank and government regulations.

Commercial loan underwriters are required to hold a bachelor's degree in business, finance, or a related field. They should also have a minimum of four to five years of experience. Underwriters should have knowledge of property valuation methods; bank and federal lending regulations; and possess excellent analytical, communication, and communication skills. Underwriters will often need to work with others to obtain missing information from the loan package. Commercial loan underwriters can earn promotions to senior underwriter, supervisor, or manager of the department. Some underwriters could choose to become trainers of new employees, while others may be able to advance their careers by obtaining more responsible positions at other firms.

Commercial Real Estate Loan Officer

Commercial loan real estate officers are responsible for originating mortgage loans for commercial properties. The properties include shopping malls, hotels, office buildings, and all types of nonresidential facilities. Commercial real estate loan officers work with the business to structure the loan so that it meets their financing needs as well as all bank and federal lending policies. They work closely with the borrower to obtain all the information needed to submit the loan for approval and serve as bank liaison throughout the life of the loan. Commercial real estate loan officers must have a bachelor's degree in business, finance, or a related field. Most employers also expect loan officers to have previous commercial banking experience, usually at least three to five years. Commercial real estate loan officers need to be able to negotiate with clients to arrive at satisfactory financing options. They should also have extensive knowledge of bank and federal lending policies and procedures.

Escrow Officer

Escrow officers are not positions that are available throughout the United States. In some states, attorneys are required to perform the same duties. Escrow officers are primarily located in the western United States. Escrow officers' primary responsibilities are to serve as an unbiased third party, review all documentation of the sale of a property, and provide all the necessary paperwork and funds required to close the deal. The escrow officer checks the title of the property and makes sure all required inspections have been performed and that each party has lived up to his or her end of the sales contract. The escrow officer will attend to such details as obtaining payoff amounts of the seller's mortgage, holding deeds, and working with legal staff. Most employers look for escrow officers who have a four-year degree or an associate's degree and several years of relevant experience. They also prefer escrow officers that have worked in the field for two to four years.

Home Inspector

The home inspector visits newly built or existing homes—usually those that are for sale and have an offer pending—to report if there are any violations of building codes, structural problems, or repairs that need to be made. Home inspectors examine every part of a home and its equipment, from the roof and chimneys to the plumbing, electrical system, furnace, and water heater. The home inspector prepares and delivers an extensive written report with recommendations for repairs and ongoing home maintenance.

Home inspectors need to have a high school diploma or equivalent. Home inspectors should also have at least a few years of experience in construction, engineering, or related fields. They need to have knowledge of building codes and requirements, construction processes, and electrical and plumbing requirements. Most states require the home inspector to be licensed. Certifications are available through the American Society of Home Inspectors (http://www .ashi.org), the National Association of Home Inspectors (http:// www.nahi.og), and the National Association of Certified Home Inspectors (http://www.nachi.org). Home inspectors can earn more money and responsibilities by acquiring the skills and knowledge needed to do more specialized inspections, such as inspections for multi-unit homes and commercial properties. Home inspectors can also open their own inspection companies.

Landscape Architect

Landscape architects design outdoor spaces for individuals, businesses, government agencies, parks, schools, and other clients. They work to design spaces that are environmentally friendly and compliant with environmental laws. Landscape architects research the area to consider all aspects of the space, meet with the client to work with him or her to create the design, and prepare the working drawings and cost estimates. A bachelor's degree or a master's degree in landscape architecture is required. In the vast majority of states a landscape architect is required to obtain a license. Most states require that the landscape architect have one to four years of experience to qualify for the license. Landscape architects should be creative, have good knowledge of plants, animals, and environmental laws where he or she practices, and possess excellent communication and organizational skills. Landscape architects are required to take continuing education classes to maintain their licenses.

Real Estate Closing Manager

The real estate closing manager works for a mortgage lender, law firm, commercial real estate company, or escrow or title company.

INTERVIEW

Staying Positive and Proactive

Diana Endjilian
Agent, Coldwell Banker Real Estate, Glendale, California

Why did you get involved in real estate?

I chose a career in real estate because I truly enjoy working with people. I was working in high-end retail prior to this. I have a passion; my passion is to be able to make people build a home out of the property that they purchase from me.

How did you structure your career path at the beginning?

I started taking real estate courses, passed the exam, and was recruited to work for the Coldwell Banker office in Glendale, California. Once joined, one of my main goals was to work toward reducing the stress people have when they think of buying or selling a property. I believe a property purchased can be used for various purposes; for example, a home to live in, rental property for income, construction, etc. For the potential client, I want to make their dreams reality by exceeding whatever it is they were looking for.

A real estate license was required to become an agent, and along with that I also studied and am now involved in other elements of the industry like short sales, BPO, and foreclosure. Also, a strong background in sales, marketing, or advertising really helps the success of your career.

I wish I had known what a great career it [real estate] can be from an earlier point in life because then I would have begun my career in real estate many years ago. I enjoy everything about the work I do and the relationships I build with people around me.

Besides the certification and license process which took about six months, education and experience is a continuous thing. Also coming in with over 25 years of sales, marketing, and advertising experience is critical in this industry because you are constantly promoting yourself and your properties. I also believe in continuous improvement and innovations, therefore I am still growing my knowledge and experience every day.

What are some of the difficulties you have experienced as a real estate agent?

Given the economy and the situation with the banks, the hardest part of my job has been when people come to me to sell their property because they simply cannot afford it. As a short sales expert, this is something I come across a lot since I also have to go and speak with people who at that time are strangers and try and help them come out of this situation and move forward with their lives. It is like being a realtor and a grief counselor, because they have to change everything in their lives.

I have had many challenges during this economic time. Seeing houses and properties in foreclosure is very devastating. Watching families move out of their homes is heartbreaking and has become one of the biggest challenges. Survival is hard when these tragic scenes are right in front of your eyes. My relationship with the people I have met in my career and personal life help me survive the emotional times the economy has placed on all people from homebuyers, sellers, colleagues, friends, and family.

What does a typical day look like for a real estate agent?
No one workday is like the one before; every day is a new and unique day with different tasks to be done. This change and variety is what I admire about my career. A typical day consists of researching properties for potential buyers that precisely meet their vision and needs, e-mailing my clients the descriptions of the properties highlighting all the pros and cons of each, scheduling appointments for the ones that they have the most interest in, and writing offers on the ones that they would like to consider purchasing. Also, for my listings and the sellers, I put together listing presentations and research comparable properties in the area (comps). I also organize marketing strategies to get my clients' properties sold in the shortest time possible so as to reduce their stress and worry about the process. The day ends very late into the night sometimes going into the next morning as I keep responding to e-mails and researching properties. It is all an ongoing process and never ever just an eight-hour day!

What advice would you give to someone just entering the field?
When sales are falling off or the market drops, the best way for an agent to survive is marketing, marketing, and more marketing. It is the key for me. Along with having the ability to change course—for instance, I decided to gain more knowledge in the short sale, BPO, and foreclosure sector, which is very demanding right now.

I look forward to obtaining my brokers license. I want to continue my career in real estate as a broker so I can be more independent and able to guide and mentor others.

If you love to work with people and cater to their needs, this is one of the most rewarding fields to be in. If you have a positive and proactive attitude, this is the perfect job since you are mostly creating your own work. Every day is a unique and rewarding challenge for me.

(continues on next page)

INTERVIEW

Staying Positive and Proactive (continued)

I subscribe to many different publications both in print and online to keep up with the latest news in real estate. The Internet is great and can be a useful tool to find articles, marketing techniques. There are also many real estate seminars to attend, which I also recommend because you are in a room with people in the same industry and it is always great to network with fellow agents too.

The closing manager prepares and obtains all of the necessary documentation for a particular commercial real estate transaction, whether it is a sale, disposition, or refinancing. He or she is responsible for making sure that all parties that are part of the transaction have met the legal and contractual arrangements of the deal. He or she then transfers the title or deed and records the change in ownership where required.

Employers prefer to hire real estate closing managers who hold bachelor's degrees in business, finance, real estate, or a related field. To become a manager the person should have at least three years of experience as a closing professional. Real estate closing managers can earn certification through the Mortgage Bankers Association of America (http://www.mbaa.org).

Relocation Counselor

Relocation counselors typically work for relocation firms. Some very large, international corporations may have their own relocation department as part of their human resources department. Relocation companies contract with corporate clients who have multiple locations throughout the United States and internationally. The counselor will work with the client's employees relocating to other cities and provide them with many services, including obtaining information on the city they are transferring to, selecting a real estate agent for them at the new city, and providing career guidance to the employee's spouse. The counselor will also help them with the sale of their current home and the transfer of all of their personal property to the new home. A bachelor's degree in real estate, business, or a related field is usually required for this position. The person may also need to have at least a few years of experience as a relocation assistant or working at a relocation company. The relocation counselor can earn many certifications through a trade association called Worldwide ERC (http://www.worldwideerc.org).

Residential Mortgage Broker

Residential mortgage brokers are independent specialists whose job entails helping a client obtain the best possible mortgage loan financing. The broker works with many different mortgage loan institutions. The residential mortgage broker is paid by commission only, and is paid by the borrower at the time of closing. The mortgage broker may be responsible for obtaining the borrower's credit reports and arranging for the property inspections and appraisals. A residential mortgage broker must have a bachelor's degree. He or she should have anywhere from two to five years of experience in mortgage banking and a very good understanding of the mortgage banking industry. States require that residential mortgage brokers are licensed. Since brokers are similar to sales representatives, they need to have excellent sales, communication, and organizational skills. Brokers need to maintain relationships with mortgage banks and institutions. Certifications are available through the National Association of Mortgage Brokers (http://www.namb.org).

Residential Mortgage Originator

Residential mortgage loan originators work at banks and other lending institutions. One of their primary responsibilities is to generate new mortgage loan business by maintaining relationships with realtors, appraisers, and others in the industry. The residential mortgage loan originator meets with the borrowers to determine whether they qualify for a loan. He or she then makes sure all necessary documentation required for underwriting is obtained. The residential mortgage loan originator is responsible for ensuring that the loan meets all bank and governmental lending requirements. He or she is also there to handle any borrower complaints, requests, or questions. Residential mortgage loan originators need to possess a bachelor's degree in real estate, finance, business, or a related field. Lending institutions look for loan originators who have at least two or three years of experience working in the mortgage loan industry. The Mortgage Bankers Association of America (http://www.mbaa .org) provides certifications for residential mortgage originators. Depending on the size and type of the lending institution, the originator may earn supervisory or management promotions within the mortgage lending department. Some successful originators may be offered the opportunity to become originators of more complicated loans such as commercial mortgage loans or construction loans.

Surveyor

Surveyors are hired by various clients to determine the legal boundaries of a particular property in question. Surveying is often done when there is a need to confirm the legal boundaries of a property, such as when an owner plans to put up a fence or add onto an existing building. Surveyors are specially trained to examine the current legal property descriptions filed with local governments that determine a property's boundaries, identify them on the plot of land, and provide new legal descriptions of the boundaries with measurements for the property owner. Surveyors will often mark the boundaries on the property for construction crews.

Surveyors are required to have a bachelor's degree. Some surveying companies provide apprenticeships for high school graduates. Surveyors must be licensed to perform surveying (unless they are serving as technicians or apprentices) and must have four years of experience before obtaining their licenses. Certifications are available through the American Congress on Surveying and Mapping (http://www.acsm.net) and the National Society of Professional Surveyors (http://www.trig-star.info). Successful surveyors can eventually become chief surveyors or field engineers. Other surveyors may choose to obtain more advanced training and education and become engineers.

Title Insurance Representative

Title insurance representatives work for title insurance companies across the United States. A title insurance policy is purchased by a lending institution or a buyer and assures them that the title (the legal document of ownership) of the property in question is free and clear, without previous liens or claims from other parties. The title insurance representative sells the title insurance policy to the customer, and then performs the work involved to see that the title is clear. Title insurance representatives spend at least half of their time pursuing sales leads, usually on the phone or meeting with potential customers. Title insurance companies prefer to hire title insurance representatives with a college degree, although some will hire reps with a high school diploma and years of experience. Like banks, title insurance companies have branches across the country, and those branches have management positions. Title insurance representatives could be promoted to those positions, eventually becoming branch managers.

Zoning Officer

The zoning officer works for a city, municipality, or county. Each city has specific zones for residential, commercial, and other uses as well as related laws. The zoning officer focuses on the zoning laws under his or her jurisdiction. He or she investigates any reports of zoning violations and takes appropriate action against the violators. The zoning officer works with citizens who wish to apply for changes in zoning and helps them prepare the required application that must go to the zoning board for approval. The zoning officer also conducts field inspections, makes zone enforcement decisions, and issues certificates of occupancy.

Most cities require their zoning officers to have a bachelor's degree in public administration, urban planning, or a related field. The zoning officer should also have at least two years of experience in reviewing and understanding site development plans. Since the zoning officer often interacts with residents and businesspeople to discuss a wide variety of claims, he or she needs to have excellent communication and interpersonal skills, as well as be a good negotiator.

Zoning officers have a few career paths to choose from, depending on the size of the city and its zoning department. Officers in smaller cities can seek transfers to larger cities, where there exists the opportunity to become a zoning administrator. This position may require master's degrees or certification, which is available through the American Association of Code Enforcement (http://www.aace1 .com). Some zoning officers may choose to find other positions in public administration.

Chapter 4

Tips for Success

Whether you are changing careers or fresh out of college, there is no doubt this is a challenging time to be starting a career in the real estate industry. However, as the industry changes to meet the needs of its customers, professionals who rise to meet these challenges will learn very important lessons which could well lead to future career successes. As many real estate pros say, if you can succeed when the economy is down, you will be successful.

It is not just the challenges or potential financial rewards that make this an attractive career choice. Its impact on the national economy—both positive and negative—make it an extremely important field to be a part of. Creative, hard-working, and innovative real estate professionals can have a positive impact when it comes to economic recovery.

When launching a career in this industry, a person will either begin as a residential agent, commercial agent, or in a related position such as a property manager. No matter what role the new employee starts out in, the person must be willing to do whatever it takes to survive and succeed. In the case of real estate agents, often that means going for several months without a paycheck, and even having to pay for his or her own business cards and marketing material.

Getting a Job in the Real Estate Industry

You have studied long and hard and have just obtained your real estate license. Now it is time to get a job. If you have been in the working world for 10 or more years and are changing careers, you will probably recall what it took to find a job when you first started out. Looking for a job used to mean spending hours scouring the want ads in newspapers. Those days are long gone. Today there are a wide range of job boards and Web sites where job seekers can search for their dream jobs. Most employers post openings on one or several sites, which can then be re-posted at other sites. If you do not have Internet access at home, it is a good idea to go to the library at least a few times a week to check for new job postings. For new real estate agents, you may have your eye on a specific brokerage firm. These firms are not always looking for new agents or may not advertise. In this case, the new agent will need to contact the real estate firm to inquire about openings.

There are also major job Web sites that are specific to real estate industry jobs, and some companies post job openings on their own Web sites. Some of the most frequently visited job Web sites today are Yahoo! HotJobs, JobCentral.com, CollegeRecruiter.com, Career-Builder.com, Monster.com, Job.com, Career.com, TrueCareers.com, Indeed.com, Net-Temps.com, JobMonkey.com, and Craigslist.org.

Web sites that are devoted to the real estate industry and post open positions include Ihirerealestate.com, Creconnection.com, Localrealestatejobs.com, and Realestatejobsite.com. Another great resource for finding jobs is through industry associations. If you are a member of an association, check that association's Web site. Chances are jobs are posted somewhere on the site, and there could be advantages to looking for jobs through an association rather than through the other sites. Often job boards are only open to members, and jobs are not posted at traditional job boards, so you are competing with a much smaller pool of people.

Do keep in mind that Web sites are not always the best way to obtain *every* job in the field. Many higher level positions may not be advertised. Job seekers for managerial or executive positions may need to contact the companies they are interested in and/or their human resources departments to learn about the company's culture and how to obtain that kind of position. Some companies offer only internal promotion while others may use third-party recruiting agencies to fill these management positions. The best way to get this information is to contact the company directly.

Finally, a great way to find open positions is through word of mouth. Just ask. If you have a friend that works at the company that you are interested in, give him or her a call and ask if there are any openings. Even if there are not openings at the time of your call, you have planted a seed in your friend's mind, so that when an opening pops up your friend will think of you. In fact, many experts argue that networking can be the best way to get a job today. According to many human resource professionals, companies are flooded with résumés for every position they advertise. Networking is a way to stand out from the crowd, which is extremely important. Recruiters recommend reaching out to previous coworkers when networking, indicating that you are exploring new opportunities.

Most companies prefer to pursue candidates recommended to them by existing employees or other professionals they know and trust. In general, hiring managers have a certain comfort level in really knowing a candidate—beyond what they learn during an interview. Having those personal referrals can go a long way in increasing your chances of getting an interview.

Today networking is not just accomplished through traditional means and relationships. Networking is also done through social Web sites such as Facebook, Twitter, and LinkedIn. As your network and interests broaden you will find others with the same interests and additional connections to others in the industry. New opportunities may come your way when you are not even looking.

If you are interested in pursuing a real estate agent position, networking may be even more important. Since the real estate industry is a very people-intensive business, and contacts which can convert to new business is critical, having recommendations from insiders in the industry is vital to convincing a brokerage you can hit the ground running with a ready list of prospects for listings and buyers.

There is another factor to be considered when looking for a job that is unique to the real estate industry. You need to know the culture of the brokerage you are considering working for. You may have your eye on the top brokerage firm in your area, but it may not always be the right choice for you. Before you apply for a position with any brokerage you need to know what kind of environment you will thrive in, and which brokerages will come closest to providing that kind of environment. For example, the top-selling firm may be highly competitive and agents may feel a great deal of pressure to earn sales. Many real estate sales professionals thrive under that kind of environment, but if it is not appealing to you, you should look elsewhere. Small brokerages may be ideal for agents just starting out if they are willing to provide a lot of one-on-one training and assistance. Some small brokerages do not have the resources to do so. Some brokerages provide a basic package of initial items the new agent might need, like business cards and brochures, while others expect the new agent to provide all of their own marketing materials.

How can you find out what kind of an environment a brokerage has? If the firm is advertising for agents, it will provide some of that information on its Web site and in the job ad. But to truly get a feel for the work environment, you should ask an agent who works there, if you can. If you do not know any agents, you can ask around or talk to someone in human resources. At the very least, you should ask to speak individually with a few agents working at the firm during the interview process before accepting a position there. Ask questions like how the agent enjoys working there, and if he or she would recommend the firm to anyone else. If the agent hesitates before answering or chooses his or her words carefully that may be a red flag. The bottom line is, you should look at a brokerage's total picture, not just how successful it is. You need to make sure that the brokerage you choose to work for supports its agents and understands how important they are to its success.

The Job Interview

Once you have applied to some open positions and landed an interview, the best policy is always to be honest about your goals, objectives, skills, and salary requirements. Like any good relationship, you are bound to find yourself mismatched with a job or company if you are not honest about what you are looking for.

Some people find themselves wondering if they are presenting themselves in the best light during job interviews. A successful job interview is both an art and a science today, especially with the ever-increasing competitiveness in today's job market. If you are unclear about how to interview well, there are a number of things you can do. First, there are many books available on the subject which can help you. Just do an Amazon.com search and you will find dozens of books written by experts which can help you hone your interviewing skills.

You should also keep in mind the basics. For example, dress well. No matter what kind of job you are seeking, you need to be professionally attired during the interview process. Assuming a relaxed or casual dress code could lead to the employer feeling that you are not serious about the job. Other experts advise to do simple things that could increase your chances of getting a second interview or the job. For example, in addition to being well-dressed, make sure you brush your teeth or use a breath mint just before the interview. If it is practical to do so, travel to the interview location prior to the day of the interview so you are familiar with how to get there and how long it takes to do so. Shake hands with the interviewer firmly. Do not sit down until the interviewer asks you to do so. You should also find the right balance of information when it comes to your answers. In other words, you need to answer the question completely, while not speaking for an unnecessarily long time or giving more information than was needed. You should ask intelligent questions about the company. This means you should do some research about it prior to the interview and have a list of questions ready. Experts also recommend that you tell the interviewer you want the job and ask about the next step in the process.

Experts also say not to chew gum during the interview, bring up controversial topics, and speak negatively of previous bosses, companies, or coworkers. It is also considered a huge mistake by experts if you smoke during an interview, even if the interviewer does and

Best
Practice

Communication

With so much information available through the Internet, television, and other media sources, people today expect instant answers to their questions. Consumers in the real estate industry are no exception. Real estate agents and brokers must be quick to respond to their clients' phone calls and e-mails. This does not mean being available 24/7, but it does mean letting clients know when to expect a response. It is standard to let clients know you will reply to any query within 24 hours. This does not mean you have to give them a definite answer, but it does mean that you should contact them to let them know that you have received their inquiry, that you are working to find the answer, and that you will call or e-mail them as soon as you have the desired information.

offers you a cigarette. Telling any kind of joke during the interview is also considered a big "no-no." Also, do not tell the interviewer you are desperate for the job or appear desperate in any way.

In the last five to 10 years many employers have begun using various tests and behavioral interviewing techniques when interviewing potential employees. These tests and techniques look at the skills required for the job, and then develop questions that assess whether the potential employee has the necessary skill levels needed. For example, since real estate agents are sales professionals, some brokerages may use tests that determine how strong the person is when it comes to his or her sales skills. Is the person good at developing prospects? Asking qualifying questions? Closing the sale? Although real estate professionals handle sales differently than other sales professionals, they must still have some sales skills in order to succeed.

Other interviewing tests and techniques may look at the candidate's customer service skills, by asking the candidate to describe a situation where he or she was challenged by a customer, and how the person handled the situation. These techniques often start with the interviewer saying the phrase: "Tell me about a time when . . . "

It is important when a candidate is interviewing for any position in real estate to be prepared for these kinds of tests and techniques. Really think about your past experiences, accomplishments, and strongest skills, and find ways to bring them to the forefront during these kinds of questions. Also be prepared to answer questions about unpleasant experiences, gaps in your employment history, and why you left your previous jobs. Always be honest. It is better to be honest than lose a job later because it is discovered you did not have the credentials you said you did.

As mentioned earlier, it is also important for people launching a career in the real estate industry to make sure they find out as much as they can about the brokerage firm before joining it. You need to know what they provide, so you have a realistic picture of what you may need to spend to get started as an agent for your marketing materials. Some brokerages do not even provide a desk and computer, the agent is expected to provide his or her own or work from home. If these kinds of considerations do not come up during the interview process, you need to ask questions so you have a complete picture of the firm before you commit to joining it. Once you have found a firm you are happy with and they make you an offer to join, it is time for the next step toward success: building a professional reputation.

Building a Professional Reputation

Once you have obtained your dream job—or the closest thing to it—in the very competitive real estate industry, you will be concerned about building a professional reputation. Most human resource professionals say that to build a professional reputation, you must look at both your external customers and internal customers. In other words, your professional reputation is built with every contact you have within the company, and outside of it. "External customers" include everyone you have contact with outside of the real estate firm or your employer. They not only include your clients, but also other people you do business with outside the firm, such as bankers, printers, and home inspectors. Keep in mind that if you have a good relationship with all of these people, when they or someone they know is looking for a real estate agent, they may turn to you. That is why it is important to conduct yourself professionally at all times. Be respectful, polite, and genuinely friendly.

Another way to build a professional reputation outside your company is to get involved in a professional organization, say some human resource professionals. The goal is to build an external network by going to seminars and conferences. Some HR pros advise professionals to be speakers or take part in professional groups where you can share your knowledge and expertise. That is another great way to build a reputation within the real estate industry.

Inside the brokerage, you need to become the "go-to" person that others will think of when opportunities arise. In the case of your internal reputation, the goal is to be as involved with the firm as you can, offering suggestions and assistance. However, experts caution that you should not overextend yourself, or this technique might backfire. Do not offer advice unless you can back it with sound knowledge and/or experience, and do not lose sight of your core duties. Make sure you are performing as an agent and are at the top of your game before branching out into other aspects of the business.

There is no getting around the fact that the real estate industry focuses on people and relationships. Some human resource professionals recommend establishing relationships with your peers within your organization. Get to know the people you work with in other departments. They say that opportunities arise when you build upon your knowledge base and get to know your associates.

In order for an up-and-coming employee or agent to create the most professional reputation possible, it is essential to have excellent communication skills. This means listening to your internal and external clients and knowing how to respond when the feedback is less than positive. Here are some tips to keep in mind when building a professional reputation:

→ **Tip #1: Use a two-step active listening technique with client problems.** Often in the real estate industry things just do not go as planned. The results can be unhappy customers and even some unhappy employees. You may be called upon to help with these situations, especially if the client is yours. Although not every problem can be easily solved, sometimes the best results occur when the client knows he or she is being heard and understood. That is where active listening comes in. If possible, take the client to a quiet location where he or she can be clearly heard. Next, listen and focus on what the person is saying. Do not interrupt or form responses in your mind while the person is speaking. Wait patiently for him or her to finish his or her thought. Finally, sum up what the person said as a first response. Start with words like these: "I want to make sure I understand what you are saying. I hear you saying that . . . " Once the client agrees that you understand what he or she said, you can propose a solution to the problem. Using this two-step format and active listening lets the client know he or she has been heard and understood. This can go a very long way to diffusing the tension in the situation, even if you cannot propose a solution that will completely "fix" it.

→ **Tip #2: Stay positive at all times when "on the job."** As mentioned, this industry is one where anything and everything can go wrong at the drop of a hat. While the temptation may exist to voice disappointment, anger, and other negative emotions, this will most likely not fix the situation, and can in fact affect others at your firm and even your client in a negative way. It certainly will not create a positive professional reputation. Instead, voice concerns with clients and other members of your firm in a way that is positive and approaches the situation from a problem-solving standpoint. For example, maybe you have a client who is complaining a great deal because it is taking longer for her house to sell than she expected it would. She may want to discuss it with the managing partner of the firm and you need to explain the situation to him or her. Instead of discussing it with the partner in terms like these: "All this client does is gripe and complain and I've done everything I know to do to sell her home," a better way to phrase it would be, "This client is unhappy because her home has not sold. Here is what I've done to market her home so far. Do you have any other ideas or suggestions?" It describes the situation accurately, presents facts, and asks for suggestions for turning the situation around but is not negative or judgmental.

→ **Tip #3: Never speak negatively about clients or other professionals in the industry.** Real estate industry professionals meet and work with a wide range of people, from mortgage bankers to developers and inspectors. It is important to create a professional reputation by keeping conversations as positive as possible, no matter how unpleasant the situation may be. That includes not making snide remarks about clients, coworkers, and managers, and competing agents at other firms, no matter how tempting. If it is the person you are talking to who starts this kind of negative conversation, the best way to handle it is to say, "I am sorry that you feel you had a negative experience with any real estate professional." Then change the subject. This acknowledges the person's feelings and opinions without agreeing or trying to delve into the situation. Grumbling to a coworker about the manager may seem like an okay thing to do at the time, but that coworker may end up becoming the boss and remember that conversation. Or the coworker may decide to tell the boss about the conversation if an opportunity presents itself. Negative conversations often have a way of coming back to haunt the participants, so the best policy is just do not have them.

→ **Tip #4: You are not "the lone ranger."** In the real estate industry, you may spend a great deal of time on your own, working with clients in the field, doing home visits, and listing their homes for sale. It may seem sometimes like you are a one-person operation. But you are not. If you are going to be successful in the extremely competitive real estate industry, you must take a team approach each day you are on the job. You rely on a vast amount of people to get a sale through to its closing. You can have skillfully negotiated a great deal, but if your buyers cannot find the right financing, it all goes down the tubes. Or perhaps your deal is smooth sailing until the home inspection, when you must work out repairs with the agent who is representing the other party in the deal. If you take a team approach to all of these necessary steps in a sale, you are much more likely to achieve that final closing. That means not taking an adversarial stance, and letting others who are part of the deal know you all want the same end

Problem
Solving

Short Sales

When it comes to residential real estate, short sales are the bane of everyone's existence. Unfortunately they are the reality of the market today, and they are not going away any time in the near future. So how do you counsel a short sale seller when the buyer walks away because the bank took too long to make a decision?

The best solution to this problem is communication. The seller needs to know you are on top of the situation and are immediately making efforts to begin marketing the property. Start scheduling visits as soon as the seller is ready. Make sure the seller knows you recognize his or her frustration and you are doing everything on your end to minimize it. When showing the home to potential buyers, be realistic about the time it may take to close on the deal. Do not recommend putting in an offer if the buyer is unsure whether he or she can wait. The good news is the government has recognized that short sales delays are hindering sales and have worked to streamline the process. In the meantime, good communication and proactive steps can minimize your seller's stress—as well as your own.

result and want to work with them to make it happen. You also may rely on others in your office to make appointments, phone clients for you, and do other administrative work. Make their jobs easier by giving them all the information they need. They are a very important part of your team. Taking a team approach in ever facet of your job is essential for your success.

➡ **Tip #5: There is no such thing as too much communication.** You listed a client's home two weeks ago. You spent quite a bit of time telling him how the process works and that it can take time to get that first appointment and offer. But already he is calling you on an almost hourly basis asking why he has not heard from you. Why? The real estate business is very detail-intense as well as people-centered. You know that when you are selling someone's home it is usually very important for it to sell as quickly as possible. People can be selling their homes for many reasons, but often they need the sale proceeds for another home or for other financial concerns. Even if there has been absolutely no action on a new listing, the agent should still communicate with the seller, letting him know what the agent is doing to market his or her house. The seller might think you put a sign up in his yard and are now sitting back and waiting for that first call. Rarely is this the case, but if you do not communicate your efforts to the seller, you could be creating that impression. You must also communicate frequently with buyers, your coworkers, and your boss. This includes attending meetings, asking questions, putting things in writing, and never assuming *anything*. Make sure information is communicated first-hand, not through a secondary source, and reiterate important details. Communicate expectations of both buyers and sellers. Keep both buyers and sellers apprised of the status of their home sale, search, or offer. Otherwise, you could end up getting a reputation as an absentee agent and lose future clients as well as the current ones.

Moving Up the Ladder

In the real estate industry there are many career paths, depending on your current position. For those in more traditional roles such as accountants and office personnel in real estate brokerage firms, you will find that getting promoted may be achieved by taking a traditional approach, such as taking on more responsibilities and handling them well. Some people think the best way to earn a promotion is by earning an MBA. Others say the best way is to find a mentor within the organization who can offer you advice and support. While neither of these methods is going to hurt your chances of getting promoted, they certainly are not going to get you there exclusively. Most executives are looking for leadership abilities when it comes to managerial and higher positions. Employees can demonstrate their leadership abilities by volunteering for new responsibilities, leading important projects, and managing volunteer work outside the scope of their jobs. Executives also look for employees with a strong work ethic. This can also be achieved by many of the same techniques listed above. It also does not hurt to ask your boss what you need to do to earn a promotion. That shows him or her that you are not afraid to take on new responsibilities and are looking to further your career. Just make sure that if he or she offers you sound advice, you take it.

For the majority of real estate professionals working as real estate agents, how you climb the ladder is going to depend on what you want to do in the future. Some agents dream of becoming managers of large offices while others want to open their own firms. Before you can take a step up, you have to know what direction you want to go. If you work for a large firm and decide you want to manage a team of agents, you will need to be highly successful as an agent first. The firm must see that you know how to be successful as an agent so you can pass on that kind of knowledge to the agents who would work under you. Then, like other management positions, you will need to be able to demonstrate that you have leadership abilities and a strong work ethic. Like others in the industry, these can be achieved by taking on new responsibilities and volunteering to lead special projects or initiatives within your firm—as long as you handle them well.

If your goal is to open your own brokerage, you will have more work to do. Similar to managing other agents, you will first have to be highly successful as an agent. Depending on the state where you reside you may also have to study for and pass additional tests by the state to become a certified broker and receive a broker's license. Then you will need to be able to attract quality agents to work for you. This may be the hardest part of opening your own brokerage. After all, if you are new you do not have an established reputation, except of your own. You may also not have the depth of resources other brokerages can offer their agents, or a specialized niche or concept within the industry. But you must have a great reputation as a top producer if you want to attract other agents to work for you. Then you will need to inspire these agents to achieve, as well as manage them and coach them when needed. Unless you have had some successful experiences managing a team of employees, you may want to take continuing education classes or gain experience as a manager before opening your own firm. There are many other factors to consider before you take the step of opening your own brokerage. Make sure you do your due diligence and talk with small business experts and others in your industry before making such a big decision.

The fact is there is no magic bullet or formulas that will ensure that you get promoted, but there are things you can do that can improve your chances and keep you top of mind so when opportunities come up you will make the list of those considered. Most human resource professionals agree that you can forget any chances of promotion if you are not competent in your current position. In fact, some say you will not even be considered unless you have proven

INTERVIEW

A Willingness to Listen

Tina Arant
Broker/Associate Manager, Watson Realty Corporation, Putnam County, Florida

What does it take to succeed in real estate?
To be a star in this industry, it takes someone who is not afraid of the word "No." It usually takes 10 rejections to find a "Yes," and you cannot quit trying to find that sale. Also, you have to be willing to say "no." If someone wants to list a property 15 to 25 percent above what the market says it should be, do not be desperate for a listing. Say no! You will show that you are the professional, that you have integrity, and that you know the market. Also, be patient. A great realtor can grow their business into a repeat and referral business, but it will take time.

Up and coming agents also need to understand the difference between a realtor and a real estate agent. Members of the National Association of Realtors get the special designation, and with it, they pledge to abide by a strict code of ethics. Whether or not you join NAR, maintaining high standards and keeping your focus on your business will help you build your business. I see too many agents who are worried about what is going wrong with the economy and focusing on the bad (even if it is not their deal), and it brings their productivity down. My mentor was willing to teach me, and I was willing to listen. You should too—do not come into a new office thinking that you know it all. None of us do. And this market is testing all of us.

Why did you choose to get involved in real estate? How did you work to advance your career?
I chose a career in real estate to have a flexible schedule as my new husband worked shift work. I also had wanted to pursue a real estate career but did not have the opportunity to do so until 2004. After becoming an agent, I continued taking real estate courses. I found I enjoyed helping other agents as much as I enjoyed helping customers find or sell their homes. So I decided to obtain a broker's license. Eventually, I decided to make a move toward management and shared my desire with my immediate supervisor as well as her regional manager. Once I qualified to become a broker, I took the real estate broker's exam and followed up with the required post-licensing

courses, which included a real estate brokers management course and a real estate investment course.

How have you managed to stay current with the real estate industry?

Prior to becoming a realtor, I spoke to a few people who had practiced real estate in the local area. When I had inquired as to what company had the best training in order to learn the business and details of taking care of customers (I was told it was Watson Realty), I neglected to inquire about the costs involved. While I knew about the cost of the initial school and license, I had no clue as to the post-license classes and association dues. Once I found out about all of the costs, I presented them to my husband (who helped me pay most of the costs) as the same amount as his "union dues." Now that I am hiring new agents or talking with people considering getting into the business, I try to prepare them up front. I let each of them know step by step what it takes to get "in the door" and how many months it can take to start seeing results. I was fortunate enough to be from a commission-only background and knew that it would be a slow start to my first payday. It officially took me about three years to gain the education and experience I needed for my present job. But every day presents new opportunities, and with the mortgage market and real estate market changes we all learn a good portion as we go. The most important thing is to know where to go to find the correct answers to a new situation. Never assume that you know it all. If you are not 100 percent sure, ask for time to find the right answer.

What are the strengths and weaknesses of a career in real estate?

I *love* being a real estate agent. The best part of my job is seeing someone succeed, no matter if it is an agent working on their first waterfront deal or a customer getting to the closing table on their first home. Also, my career meets the needs of my family. I have the income that I need, the support of a great company, and a wonderful husband.

The worst part of my job is having to break the news to someone that they cannot close on a home that they had their heart set on. Many of the current buyers are first timers. It takes a while for them to find the "comfort zone" of finding a home, negotiating the deal, and getting through inspections and financing requirements. Having to go to them and let them know that something went wrong is heart wrenching.

yourself competent in your present position. Once it is clear you have mastered your current level, there are actions you can take and things to avoid that will increase your chances of getting a promotion. Some HR professionals advise employees to look at the job they want and the skills it requires. Most likely there will be skill sets that you either do not have, or have not been able to prove that you have. Managers are more likely to promote employees that take the initiative to acquire the skills that appear to be missing.

If the job you want requires very different skills and you are working in a large organization with lots of developmental programs in place, you may have to take the time to develop them on your own through continuing education or online classes. You can also show decision makers you are willing to take on leadership assignments and prove you are willing to invest in yourself through training, reading, and education.

Some human resources experts also recommend working with your current supervisor to develop a strategy that will lead to the job you are eyeing. It is also a good idea to find a mentor in the department you want to be promoted into. However, do not rely on mentoring alone. Mentoring will only work if you have proven yourself capable in your current position, and are working to prove you have the skills required to move to the next level.

In *The Realities of Management Promotion: An Investigation of Factors Influencing the Promotion of Managers in Three Major Companies,* authors Marian N. Ruderman and Patricia J. Ohlott looked at why promotions occurred at three Fortune 500 companies. They looked at 64 promotions that were considered typical at the companies and asked what had led to the promotions. Their research indicates that the promotions were based on the individuals' efforts and abilities. They found that jobs were often created to fit the candidate. The decision makers did not place much emphasis on formal assessments, such as performance evaluations. They found that in almost half of the cases only one person was considered for the job. In addition, a tremendous variety existed among the types of promotions. The bottom line of the research was that organizational context should be considered when trying to understand promotions. In other words, spend time to really understand your firm's culture and the process used to hire and promote. Each firm will be different. Ask questions and do your research.

Here is a list of dos and do nots developed by Elizabeth Freedman, MBA, an award-winning speaker and business columnist and author of *Work 101: Learning the Ropes of the Workplace without Hanging*

Yourself and *The MBA Student's Job-Seeking Bible*. Some of her recommendations for people seeking promotions are

➡ Do imitate those who have the job you want. Take them out to coffee or lunch and ask questions about what qualities have made them successful on the job.

➡ Do become an expert in your field. Join industry associations and groups and attend their meetings and seminars even if you have to pay for them yourself. The education and networking you will experience will be worth every penny of the investment and make you more marketable to your company and others.

➡ Understand your boss and his or her priorities. When you see how your job fits in with your boss's and prioritize your work in conjunction with his or hers you make your boss look good. And in turn you will look good. It will also help you to understand when the best time is to ask her questions or when he needs to be left alone. These kinds of considerations go a long way.

➡ Make an effort to get along with all coworkers no matter how old they are. This is especially true in the real estate industry, where coworkers can be anywhere from 18 to 65. We all tend to gravitate toward people our own age or think of younger people as our kids or older people as our parents. But when you work with people of different age ranges it is important to put those tendencies aside and find common ground. A real estate firm has to work together as a team if it is going to function smoothly and for the success of all involved. So remember you are all on the same team and try to get along.

➡ Do not try to fight the current system. Even if you clearly see some of its inefficiencies, the best way to correct them is working with the system rather than against it. Making suggestions for improvements is a positive way to initiate needed changes. Remember where you are in the hierarchy and work within the scope of your position as you try to make things more efficient.

➡ Do not forget that you and your work are always visible. It may seem sometimes like no one is paying attention or a particular task is not important, but performing sloppily will always come back to haunt you. It may also be that the task you thought no one cared about was the one task management is watching to determine if you are manager material. Always perform at your best and view every project as an opportunity to show your stuff.

➡ Do not get the reputation as a complainer. You may be entirely correct about the problems within the organization, but if you take every opportunity to complain about them rather than taking a more positive approach you will be seen as the complainer instead of the person with great ideas for improvement. Freedman says you might also be seen as someone who is not knowledgeable enough about the company or the industry to know what works and what does not. The best way to proceed when things just are not "right" in your eyes is to do your research, ask questions, and make suggestions to decision makers. Keep your complaints private.

➡ Do not become invisible. You may be overwhelmed with work, but if you bury yourself and do not volunteer to help others or make a real effort to connect with coworkers on a regular basis your name will not be one of the first mentioned when an opportunity comes along.

Planning Your Career in the Real Estate Industry

Like getting a promotion, there is no "right" way to plan your career in the real estate industry—or any other, for that matter. Experts agree that it is most important for you to know what you really want, and then work with key people to develop a plan to get there.

For some that may be the easy part. For others it is not so easy. Some career experts say there have been numerous cases of people spending years pursuing a specific career only to land that dream job and realize it was not what they thought it was at all. Before you find yourself in that position, if you have not already done so, spend some time in the area of the industry you have chosen. Talk to people who are already where you want to be and ask them lots of questions. Make sure the career path you are choosing is really going to give you the end results you are looking for. You have to have self-awareness and initiative when planning your career, and know exactly what it is you want.

So once you have determined what you want, then what? How do you go about realizing your dreams? First you need to make sure your goals are realistic. For example, not everyone can be the CEO, but perhaps the director or VP is a more suitable role for a particular person or skill level. Then depending on your ultimate goal and your current position, you have a few options. If you are employed by a larger company with a human resources department, you can meet with a professional in that department to discuss your career goals and develop a career plan. At some companies, your manager will be responsible for working with you to develop your plan. Either way, you should work with someone at the firm who has been there long enough to know the culture and can assist you in developing your career.

Just as you did when working toward a promotion, look at the skills required for your ultimate goal and then at the skills you currently possess. If you are missing some basic skills, take it upon yourself to develop them, either through your company and the training it has to offer or through other educational opportunities like college courses and continuing education through industry associations. It is also important to continue to stay in touch with industry trends, company culture, and opportunities inside and outside your current scope of responsibilities. You will be more likely to reach your ultimate goal, enjoy it, and succeed if you do.

Fast Facts

More Single Women Are Buying Homes

In the summer of 2009, the National Association of Realtors surveyed home buyers about their experience with the home search process and the use of real estate professionals in purchasing a home. One of the results indicates that the number of single women buying homes has increased dramatically. The percentage of single female buyers increased from 14 percent in 1995 to 21 percent in 2009. In fact, says NAR, single females account for the second largest demographic of adult households who purchase homes.

Continuing Education and Certifications

You already know that to become a real estate agent or broker, you must earn a license. Additionally, the National Association of Realtors offers continuing education and certifications for member agents. Some brokerages prefer to hire real estate agents with these certifications.

The U.S. Bureau of Labor Statistics notes that most universities, colleges, and community colleges offer various courses in real estate. Some offer associate and bachelor's degrees in real estate, but mostly they offer certificate programs. Additionally, college courses in finance, business administration, statistics, economics, law, and English are also helpful. For those who intend to start their own company, business courses such as marketing and accounting are as important as courses in real estate or finance.

There are local real estate associations that are members of the National Association of Realtors which sponsor courses covering the basics as well as some essential details of the industry. You can also take advanced courses in mortgage financing, property development and management, and other subjects through these local associations. Also, some brokerage firms do offer formal training programs for new and experienced agents.

Licensure is not optional. According to the Bureau, in every state and the District of Columbia, real estate brokers and sales agents must be licensed. Any person who wants to work as an agent or a broker must pass a written examination. The examination is more comprehensive for brokers than for agents and includes questions on basic real estate transactions and the laws affecting the sale of property. Most states require candidates for the general sales license to complete between 30 and 90 hours of classroom instruction. To get a broker's license an individual needs at least 60 to 90 hours of formal training and a certain amount of experience selling real estate, usually one to three years. Some states waive the experience requirements for the broker's license if the applicant holds a bachelor's degree in real estate.

Once you have your license you are not finished. State licenses typically must be renewed every one or two years, although usually no examination is needed. However, many states require continuing education for license renewals. The Bureau recommends contacting the real estate licensing commission of your state to verify your exact licensing requirements.

Generally speaking, most employees in the industry can get certifications related to their field through an industry association. For example, if you are a public relations coordinator for a large brokerage, you can get certification through the Public Relations Society of America. Professionals in certain fields, such as information technology, must be certified in software and management programs to land particular jobs. Before you take the time and spend the money to earn a certification, talk to managers and HR professionals to make sure it will truly benefit you. To determine whether you need certification and continuing education, it is always best to rely on your human resources professional and the culture in your company.

Chapter 5

Talk Like a Pro

Many people new to real estate get very anxious when they hear their colleagues speaking what sounds like a completely different language. In this industry, there is a lot to learn, and vocabulary is just one aspect of the education you will need. To give you a head start, we present the following glossary of real estate terms. Study this, and you will sound like a pro in short order.

401(k)/403(b)   An employer-sponsored investment plan that allows individuals to set aside tax-deferred income for retirement or emergency purposes. A 401(k) plan is provided by employers that are private corporations. A 403(b) plan is provided by employers that are not-for-profit organizations.

401(k)/403(b) loan   Some administrators of 401(k)/403(b) plans allow for loans against the monies you have accumulated in these plans. Loans against 401(k) plans are an acceptable source of down payment for most types of loans.

A, B, C, or D paper   Mortgage loans are rated as A, B, C, or D paper. "A" paper loans are the highest-quality loans and present the lowest risk; "B" loans involve borrowers with minor credit problems; "C" quality are for borrowers with marginal or poor credit; "D" paper loans carry very high risk.

absorption rate   The total number of vacant square feet of office space divided by the square footage leased per year historically, used to analyze demand of office space in a given market area. Can also analyze real-estate property demand in general by taking the total number of available properties and dividing the figure by the number of properties sold per year historically.

acceleration clause   A clause in a mortgage that allows the lender to demand payment of an outstanding loan balance. The most common reasons for accelerating a loan are a default on the loan or if a buyer transfers title to another entity without informing the lender.

accord and satisfaction   The settlement of an obligation. An accord is an agreement by a creditor to accept less than bargained for from a debtor. The creditor's acceptance of the accord constitutes satisfaction of the debt.

accounting   The reporting of the status of all funds received from or on behalf of a property buyer. Most state real estate license laws require a broker to give accurate copies of all documents to all parties affected by them and to keep copies on file for a specified period of time. Most license laws also require the broker to deposit all money entrusted to him or her into a special trust or escrow account immediately, or within 24 to 48 hours. Mixing those funds with the broker's personal or general business funds is unethical and illegal.

acknowledgment   A formal declaration made before a duly authorized officer, usually a notary public, by a person who has signed a document; also, the document itself. An acknowledgment is designed to keep forged and fraudulently induced documents from taking effect.

adjustable-rate mortgage (ARM)   A mortgage in which the interest rate changes periodically, based on corresponding fluctuations in an index.

adjusted basis   The original cost basis of a property reduced by the amount of allowable depreciation (decrease in value) or depletion allowances (a tax deduction authorized by federal law for the exhaustion of oil and gas wells, mines, timber, mineral deposits or reserves, and other natural deposits) taken and the amount of any unpaid property losses suffered and increased by the cost of capital improvements plus certain carrying costs and assessments. The amount of gain or loss recognized upon sale of a property is determined by subtracting the adjusted basis on the date of sale from the adjusted sales price.

adjustment date   The date the interest rate changes on an adjustable-rate mortgage.

amortization   The portion of the loan payment applied to pay accruing interest on a loan, with the remainder being applied to the principal. Over time, the interest portion decreases as the loan balance falls, and the amount is applied to principal increases so that the loan is paid off (amortized) in the specified time.

amortization schedule   A table which breaks down the amount of a loan payment to be applied toward the principal and the amount allocated to interest over the life of the loan. Visually, it shows how the loan balance gradually falls until reaching zero.

annual percentage rate (APR)   Determined by a government formula, APR is a percentage figure that shows the true annual cost of a loan.

appraisal   A written justification of the price paid for a property, primarily based on an analysis of comparable sales of similar structures in the area.

appraised value   An estimate of a property's fair market value, based on an appraiser's knowledge, experience, and property analysis.

appraiser   An individual qualified by education, training, and experience to estimate the value of real property and personal property. Many appraisers work directly for mortgage lenders, but most operate as independent contractors.

appreciation   An increase in a property's value due to changes in market conditions, inflation, or other causes.

assessed value   The worth of a property as determined by a government tax assessor.

assessment   The placing of a value on property for tax purposes.

assessor   A government official who establishes a property's value for tax purposes.

assets   Items of value owned by an individual, collective, or company. Liquid assets are those that can be converted quickly into cash, among them bank accounts, stocks, and bonds. Other assets include real estate, personal property, and debts owed to an individual by others.

assignment   The transfer of ownership of a mortgage from one company or individual to another.

assumable mortgage   A mortgage that can be taken over by a buyer when a property is sold.

assumption   When a buyer assumes a seller's mortgage.

balloon mortgage   A mortgage loan that requires the remaining principal balance be paid at a specific point in time. For example, a loan may be amortized as if it would be paid over a 30-year period, but requires that the entire remaining balance be paid at the end of the 10th year.

balloon payment   The final lump sum payment due at the end of a balloon mortgage.

bankruptcy   A drastic legal move made in federal court allowing an individual or company to restructure or discharge outstanding debts.

bill of sale   A written document transferring title to personal property.

biweekly mortgage   A mortgage in which payments are made every two weeks rather than the standard once per month. Biweekly payments result in the equivalent of 13 monthly payments over the course of a calendar year, which helps reduce the time it takes to pay off a 30-year mortgage.

bond market   Usually refers to the daily buying and selling of 30-year treasury bonds. This volatile, rapidly changing market is extremely important to mortgage lenders, because as bond yields rise or fall, so do fixed-rate mortgages.

Professional
Ethics

Positions of Trust

Real estate agents and brokers of both commercial and residential segments are often privy to their clients' personal and confidential information. Additionally, real estate professionals are put in positions of trust. It is the client's desire that his or her real estate professional is looking after his or her best interest. If a real estate professional is to remain in business and successful for the long-term, he or she must behave ethically. The National Association of Realtors provides a stringent code of ethics to which its members must adhere. To view this code of ethics, go to the NAR Web site at http://www.realtor.org/mem polweb.nsf/pages/code.

bridge loan Loans obtained by homeowners who have not yet sold their previous property, but need to close on a new purchase. The bridge loan covers the down payment for the new property.

broker Anyone who acts as an agent, bringing two parties together for any type of transaction and earns a fee for doing so. Most realtors are "agents" who work under a "broker." Some agents are brokers as well, either working for themselves or under another broker. In the mortgage industry, broker usually refers to a company or individual that does not lend the money for the loans themselves, but broker loans to larger lenders or investors.

broker price opinion (BPO) A method that a real estate broker or sales agent uses to estimate the likely selling price of a real estate property. The estimate of price is submitted in a BPO report that includes local and regional market information, neighborhood analysis, and comparable properties that compare to the house being evaluated.

buydown A financing technique used to reduce the monthly payments for the first few years of a loan. Funds in the form of discount points are given to the lender by the builder or seller to buy down or lower the effective interest rate paid by the buyer, thus reducing the monthly payments for a set time.

call option Similar to the acceleration clause.

canceling escrow Providing written notification that an escrow is to be terminated; must be done by mutual consent of all parties to the escrow and in accordance with governing agreements.

cap Yearly and/or life-of-loan limitations on the amount of variation allowed when adjusting interest on variable-rate loans.

capacity of parties The legal ability of people or organizations to enter into a valid contract. A person entering into a contract will have full, limited, or no capacity to contract.

capital gain Profit earned from the sale of an asset, where the sales price was greater than the adjusted basis.

capitalization A formula for converting net income into an indication of value. The net income of the property is divided by an appropriate (capitalization) rate of return to give the indicated value. (Income ÷ Rate = Value)

capitalization rate The rate of return a property will produce on the owner's investment.

capital loss   Loss sustained from the sale of an asset, where the sales price is less than the adjusted book basis. *See* adjusted basis.

cash-out refinance   When a borrower refinances a mortgage at a higher amount than the value of the current loan balance with the intention of pulling out money for personal use.

certificate of deposit   A time deposit held in a bank that pays a certain amount of interest to the depositor.

certificate of deposit index   One of the indexes used for determining interest rate changes on some adjustable rate mortgages; it uses an average of what banks are paying currently on certificates of deposit.

Certificate of Eligibility   A document issued by the Veterans Administration that certifies eligibility for a VA loan.

Certificate of Reasonable Value (CRV)   Issued once an appraisal has been performed on a property being bought with a VA loan.

chain of title   An analysis of the transfers of title to a piece of property over time.

clear title   A title that is free of liens or legal questions as to property ownership.

closing   In some states a real estate transaction is not considered "closed" until the documents record at the local recorders' office. In others, the "closing" is a meeting where all of a real estate deal's documents are signed and money changes hands.

closing costs   Closing costs are the final fees paid to transfer ownership of a real estate property. The fees separated into two types: "non-recurring closing costs" and "pre-paid items." Non-recurring closing costs are items paid for just once during the process of buying the property or obtaining a loan. "Pre-paid" items are those which recur over time; for instance, property taxes and homeowners insurance. A lender makes an attempt to estimate the amount of non-recurring closing costs and prepaid items on a Good Faith Estimate, which must be given to the borrower within three days of receiving a home loan application.

closing statement   *See* settlement statement

cloud on title   Any conditions revealed by a title search that negatively impacts a real estate title. Clouds on title generally cannot be removed except by deed, release, or court action.

co-borrower   An additional individual who is both obligated on the loan and whose name is on the property title.

collateral   In a home loan, the property is the collateral. The borrower risks losing the property if the loan is not repaid according to the terms of the mortgage or deed of trust.

collateralized debt obligation   A type of structured asset-backed security whose value and payments are derived from a portfolio of fixed-income underlying assets that can carry huge risk.

collection   When a borrower falls behind in his or her payments, the lender contacts them in an effort to bring the loan current. The loan goes to "collection," at which point the lender must mail and record certain documents in case they are eventually required to foreclose on the property.

commission   Payment to a broker for services rendered in the sale or purchase of real property; usually a percentage of the property's selling price.

common area assessments   Also known in some areas as Homeowners Association Fees, these are charges paid to a Homeowners Association by the owners of the individual units in a condominium or planned unit development; generally used to maintain the property and common areas.

common areas   Those portions of a building, land, and amenities owned (or managed) by a planned unit development or condominium project's homeowners' association (or a cooperative project's cooperative corporation) that are used by all of the unit owners, who share in the common expenses of their operation and maintenance. Common areas include swimming pools, tennis courts, and other recreational facilities, as well as common corridors of buildings and parking areas.

common law   An unwritten body of law based on general custom in England and used to an extent in some states.

community property   A system of property ownership giving spouses an equal interest in the property acquired by the efforts of either spouse during their marriage.

comparable sales   Recent sales of similar properties in nearby areas; used to help determine a property's market value. Also referred to as "comps."

condominium   A type of ownership in real property where all of the owners own the property, common areas, and buildings together, with the exception of the interior of the unit to which they have title. Often mistakenly referred to as a type of construction or development, it actually refers to the type of ownership. Each condominium unit is a statutory entity that may be mortgaged, taxed, sold, or otherwise transferred in ownership, separately and independently of all other units in the condo project. The unit also can be foreclosed upon separately, in case of default on the mortgage note or other lienable payments.

condominium conversion   Changing the ownership of an existing building (usually a rental project) to the condominium form of ownership.

condominium hotel   A condominium project that has rental or registration desks, short-term occupancy, food and telephone services, and daily cleaning services and that is operated as a commercial hotel even though the units are individually owned. These are often found in resort areas like Hawaii.

construction loan   A short-term, interim loan for financing the cost of construction. The lender makes payments to the builder at periodic intervals as the work progresses.

constructive fraud   Breach of a legal or equitable duty that the law declares fraudulent because of its tendency to deceive others, despite no showing of dishonesty or intent to deceive. A broker may be charged with constructive fraud for failing to disclose a known material fact when the broker had a duty to speak—for example, if a listing broker failed to disclose a known major foundation problem not readily observable upon an ordinary inspection.

contingency   A condition that must be met before a contract is legally binding. Homebuyers often include a contingency that specifies that the contract is not binding until the purchaser obtains a satisfactory home inspection report from a qualified inspector.

continuing education   A requirement in most states that real estate and appraiser licensees complete a specified number of educational offerings as a prerequisite to license renewal or reinstatement.

contract   A legally enforceable promise or set of promises that must be performed and for which, if breached, the law provides a remedy.

conventional mortgage   Refers to home loans other than government loans (VA and FHA).

convertible ARM   An adjustable-rate mortgage that allows the borrower to change the ARM to a fixed-rate mortgage within a specific time.

cooperative (co-op)   A type of multiple ownership in which the residents of a multi-unit housing complex own shares in the cooperative corporation that owns the property, giving each resident the right to occupy a specific unit.

cost of funds index (COFI)   One of the indexes used to determine interest rate changes for certain adjustable-rate mortgages. It represents the weighted-average (involves the assignment of different levels of importance or weights) cost of savings, borrowings, and advances of the financial institutions such as banks and savings and loans and is calculated and reported by the Federal Home Loan Bank of San Francisco. The entire index name is 11th District Monthly Weighted Average Cost of Funds Index.

credit   An agreement in which a borrower receives something of value in exchange for a promise to repay the lender at a later date.

credit history   A record of an individual's repayment of debt. Credit histories are reviewed my mortgage lenders as one of the underwriting criteria in determining credit risk.

creditor   A person to whom money is owed.

credit report   A report of an individual's credit history prepared by a credit bureau and used by a lender in determining a loan applicant's creditworthiness.

credit repository   An organization that gathers, records, updates, and stores financial and public records information about the payment records of individuals who are being considered for credit.

debt   An amount owed to another.

deed   The legal document conveying title to a property.

deed-in-lieu   Short for "deed in lieu of foreclosure," this conveys title to the lender when the borrower is in default and wants to avoid foreclosure. The lender may or may not cease foreclosure activities if a borrower asks to provide a deed-in-lieu. Regardless of whether the lender accepts the deed-in-lieu, the avoidance and non-repayment of debt will most likely show on a credit history. What a deed-in-lieu may prevent is having the documents preparatory to a foreclosure being recorded and become a matter of public record.

deed of trust   Some states, like California, do not record mortgages. Instead, they record a deed of trust, which is essentially the same thing.

Everyone

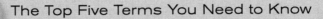

Knows

The Top Five Terms You Need to Know

1. **earnest money deposit:** A deposit made by the potential homebuyer to show that he or she is serious about buying the house.

2. **equity:** A homeowner's financial interest in a property. Equity is the difference between the fair market value of the property and the amount still owed on its mortgage and other liens.

3. **purchase agreement:** A written contract signed by the buyer and seller stating the terms and conditions under which a property will be sold.

4. **realtor:** A real estate agent, broker, or associate who holds active membership in a local real estate board that is affiliated with the National Association of Realtors.

5. **Truth-in-Lending:** A federal law that requires lenders to fully disclose, in writing, the terms and conditions of a mortgage, including the annual percentage rate (APR), and other charges.

default   Failure to make the mortgage payment within a specified period of time. For first mortgages or first trust deeds, if a payment has still not been made within 30 days of the due date, the loan is considered to be in default.

delinquency   Failure to make mortgage payments when mortgage payments are due. For most mortgages, payments are due on the first day of the month. Even though they may not charge a "late fee" for a number of days, the payment is still considered to be late and the loan delinquent. When a loan payment is more than 30 days late, most lenders report the late payment to one or more credit bureaus.

deposit   A sum of money given in advance of a larger amount being expected in the future. Often referred to as an "earnest money deposit."

depreciation   A decline in the value of property; the opposite of appreciation. Depreciation is also an accounting term which shows the declining monetary value of an asset and is used as an expense to reduce taxable income. Since this is not a true expense where money is actually paid, lenders will add back depreciation expense for self-employed borrowers and count it as income.

discount points   In the mortgage industry, this term is usually used only in reference to government loans, meaning FHA and VA loans. Discount points refer to any "points" paid in addition to the 1 percent loan origination fee. A "point" is 1 percent of the loan amount.

down payment   The part of the purchase price of a property that the buyer pays in cash and does not finance with a mortgage.

due-on-sale provision   A provision in a mortgage that allows the lender to demand repayment in full if the borrower sells the property that serves as security for the mortgage.

earnest money deposit   A deposit made by the potential homebuyer to show that he or she is serious about buying the house.

easement   A right of way giving persons other than the owner access to or over a property.

effective age   An appraiser's estimate of the physical condition of a building. The actual age of a building may be shorter or longer than its effective age.

eminent domain   The right of a government to take private property for public use upon payment of its fair market value. Eminent domain is the basis for condemnation proceedings.

encroachment   An improvement that intrudes illegally on another's property.

encumbrance   Anything that affects or limits the fee simple title to a property, such as mortgages, leases, easements, or restrictions.

Equal Credit Opportunity Act (ECOA)   A federal law that requires lenders and other creditors to make credit equally available without discrimination based on race, color, religion, national origin, age, sex, marital status, or receipt of income from public assistance programs.

equity   A homeowner's financial interest in a property. Equity is the difference between the fair market value of the property and the amount still owed on its mortgage and other liens.

escheat   When property and/or an estate is transferred to the government because its owner has died without a will or an heir to his or her estate. Transferred property can be claimed back by relatives through the court system.

escrow   An item of value, money, or documents deposited with a third party to be delivered upon the fulfillment of a condition. For example, the earnest money deposit is put into escrow until delivered to the seller when the transaction is closed.

escrow account   Once you close your purchase transaction, you may have an escrow account or impound account with your lender. This means the amount you pay each month includes an amount above what would be required if you were only paying your principal and interest. The extra money is held in your impound account (escrow account) for the payment of items like property taxes and homeowner's insurance when they come due. The lender pays them with your money instead of you paying them yourself.

escrow analysis   Once each year your lender will perform an "escrow analysis" to make sure they are collecting the correct amount of money for the anticipated expenditures.

escrow disbursements   The use of escrow funds to pay real estate taxes, hazard insurance, mortgage insurance, and other property expenses as they become due.

estate   The ownership interest of an individual in real property. The sum total of all the real property and personal property owned by an individual at time of death.

eviction   The lawful expulsion of an occupant from real property.

examination of title   The report on the title of a property from the public records or an abstract of the title.

exclusive listing   A written contract that gives a licensed real estate agent the exclusive right to sell a property for a specified time.

executor   A person named in a will to administer an estate. The court will appoint an administrator if no executor is named. "Executrix" is the feminine form.

Fair Credit Reporting Act   A consumer protection law that regulates the disclosure of consumer credit reports by consumer/credit reporting agencies and establishes procedures for correcting mistakes on one's credit record.

fair market value   The highest price that a buyer, willing but not compelled to buy, would pay, and the lowest a seller, willing but not compelled to sell, would accept.

Fannie Mae (FNMA)   The Federal National Mortgage Association, which is a congressionally chartered, shareholder-owned company that is the nation's largest supplier of home mortgage funds.

Fannie Mae's Community Homebuyer's Program An income-based community lending model, under which mortgage insurers and Fannie Mae offer flexible underwriting guidelines to increase a low- or moderate-income family's buying power and to decrease the total amount of cash needed to purchase a home. Borrowers who participate in this model are required to attend pre-purchase homebuyer education sessions.

Federal Housing Administration (FHA) An agency of the U.S. Department of Housing and Urban Development (HUD). Its main activity is the insuring of residential mortgage loans made by private lenders. The FHA sets standards for construction and underwriting, but does not lend money or plan or construct housing.

fee simple The greatest possible ownership interest a person can have in real estate.

fee simple estate An unconditional, unlimited estate of inheritance that represents the greatest estate and most extensive interest in land that can be enjoyed. It is of perpetual duration. When the real estate is in a condominium project, the unit owner is the exclusive owner only of the air space within his or her portion of the building (the unit) and is an owner in common with respect to the land and other common portions of the property.

FHA mortgage A mortgage that is insured by the Federal Housing Administration (FHA). Along with VA loans, an FHA loan will often be referred to as a government loan.

firm commitment A lender's agreement to make a loan to a specific borrower on a specific property.

first mortgage The mortgage that is in first place among any loans recorded against a property. Usually refers to the date in which loans are recorded, but there are exceptions.

fixed-rate mortgage A mortgage in which the interest rate does not change during the entire term of the loan.

fixture Personal property that becomes real property when attached in a permanent manner to real estate.

flood insurance Insurance that compensates for physical property damage resulting from flooding. It is required for properties located in federally designated flood areas.

foreclosure The legal process by which a borrower in default under a mortgage is deprived of his or her interest in the mortgaged property. This usually involves a forced sale of the property at public auction with the proceeds of the sale being applied to the mortgage debt.

Freddie Mac (FHLMC)   The Federal Home Loan Mortgage Corporation is a stockholder-owned corporation chartered by Congress in 1970 to keep money flowing to mortgage lenders in support of homeownership and rental housing.

government loan (mortgage)   A mortgage that is insured by the Federal Housing Administration (FHA) or guaranteed by the Department of Veterans Affairs (VA) or the Rural Housing Service (RHS). Mortgages that are not government loans are classified as conventional loans.

Government National Mortgage Association (Ginnie Mae)   A government-owned corporation within the U.S. Department of Housing and Urban Development (HUD). Created by Congress on September 1, 1968, GNMA performs the same role as Fannie Mae and Freddie Mac in providing funds to lenders for making home loans. The difference is that Ginnie Mae provides funds for government loans (FHA and VA).

grantee   The person to whom an interest in real property is conveyed.

grantor   The person conveying an interest in real property.

hazard insurance   Insurance that offers coverage in the event of physical damage to a property from fire, wind, vandalism, or other hazards.

Home Equity Conversion Mortgage (HECM)   Usually referred to as a reverse annuity mortgage, by using this instrument the lender makes payments to the buyer rather than the other way around. A reverse mortgage enables older homeowners to convert the equity they have in their homes into cash, usually in the form of monthly payments. Unlike traditional home equity loans, a borrower does not qualify on the basis of income but on the value of his or her home. In addition, the loan does not have to be repaid until the borrower no longer occupies the property; repayment usually comes from the proceeds of the borrower's estate.

home equity line of credit   A mortgage loan that allows the borrower to obtain cash drawn against the equity of his home, up to a predetermined amount.

home inspection   A thorough inspection by a professional that evaluates the structural and mechanical condition of a property.

A satisfactory home inspection is generally require before a deal can close.

homeowners' association   A nonprofit association that manages the common areas of a planned unit development (PUD) or condominium project. In a condominium project, it has no ownership interest in the common elements. In a PUD project, the association legally owns these common spaces.

homeowner's insurance   An insurance policy that combines personal liability insurance and hazard insurance coverage for a domicile and what is inside.

homeowner's warranty   A type of insurance often purchased by homebuyers that covers repairs to certain items, such as heating or air conditioning, if they malfunction within the coverage period. It can be bought by either the buyer or the seller.

HUD median income   Median family income for a particular county or metropolitan statistical area (MSA), as estimated by the Department of Housing and Urban Development (HUD).

HUD-1 settlement statement   A document that provides an itemized listing of the funds that are paid at closing. Items that appear on the statement include real estate commissions, loan fees, points, and initial escrow (impound) amounts. Each type of expense goes on a specific numbered line on the sheet. The totals at the bottom of the HUD-1 statement define the seller's net proceeds and the buyer's net payment at closing. It is called a HUD1 because the form is printed by the Department of Housing and Urban Development (HUD). The HUD1 statement is also known as the "closing statement" or "settlement sheet."

joint tenancy   A form of ownership or taking title to property, which means each party owns the whole property and that ownership is not separate. In the event of the death of one party, the survivor owns the property in its entirety.

judgment   A decision made by a court of law. In judgments that require the repayment of a debt, the court may place a lien against the debtor's real property as collateral for the judgment's creditor.

judicial foreclosure   A type of foreclosure proceeding used in some states that is handled as a civil lawsuit and conducted entirely under the auspices of a court. Other states use non-judicial foreclosure.

jumbo loan   A loan that exceeds Fannie Mae's and Freddie Mac's loan limits, currently at $227,150. Also called a nonconforming loan. Freddie Mac and Fannie Mae loans are referred to as conforming loans.

late charge   The penalty a borrower must pay when a payment is made a stated number of days. On a first trust deed or mortgage, this is usually 15 days.

lease   A written agreement between the property owner and a tenant that stipulates the payment and conditions under which the tenant may possess the real estate for a specified period of time.

leasehold estate   A way of holding title to a property wherein the mortgagor does not actually own the property, but rather has a recorded long-term lease on it.

lease option   An alternative financing option that allows homebuyers to lease a home with an option to buy. Each month's rent payment may consist of not only the rent, but an additional amount which can be applied toward the down payment on an already specified price.

legal description   A property description, recognized by law, that is sufficient to locate and identify the property without oral testimony.

lender   A term which can refer to the institution making the loan or to the individual representing the firm. For example, loan officers are often referred to as "lenders."

liabilities   A person's financial obligations. Liabilities include long-term and short-term debt, as well as any other amounts that are owed to others.

liability insurance   Insurance coverage that offers protection against claims alleging that a property owner's negligence or inappropriate action resulted in bodily injury or property damage to another party. It is usually part of a homeowner's insurance policy.

lien   A legal claim against a property that must be paid off when the property is sold. A mortgage or first trust deed is considered a lien.

life cap   For an adjustable-rate mortgage (ARM), a limit on the amount that the interest rate can increase or decrease over the life of the mortgage.

line of credit   An agreement by a commercial bank or other financial institution to extend credit up to a certain amount for a certain time to a specified borrower.

liquid asset   A cash asset or an asset that is easily converted into cash.

On the Cutting Edge

Green Homes

Researchers at the National Association of Realtors and the National Association of Home Builders say that "green homes," those that are built with environmentally friendly materials or use environmentally friendly and resource conserving technologies, may have a competitive edge over traditional homes when it comes to home sales. In the future, homes that are already sensitive to environmental concerns will be more attractive to buyers than homes that are not. According to the National Association of Home Builders, more than 97,000 homes have been built and certified by voluntary green building programs around the country since the mid-1990s, representing a 50 percent increase from the survey conducted in 2004. Also, more than half of NAHB's 235,000 members (representing about 80 percent of homebuilders) say they expect to use at least some green building practices by the end of the year.

loan A sum of borrowed money (principal) that is generally repaid with interest.

loan officer Also referred to by a variety of other terms, such as lender, loan representative, loan "rep," account executive, and others. The loan officer serves several functions and has various responsibilities: they solicit loans, they are the representative of the lending institution, and they represent the borrower to the lending institution.

loan origination How a lender refers to the process of obtaining new loans.

loan servicing After you obtain a loan, the company you make the payments to is "servicing" your loan. They process payments, send statements, manage the escrow/impound account, provide collection efforts on delinquent loans, ensure that insurance and property taxes are made on the property, handle pay-offs and assumptions, and provide a variety of other services.

loan-to-value (LTV)   The percentage relationship between the amount of the loan and the appraised value or sales price (whichever is lower).

lock-in   An agreement in which the lender guarantees a specified interest rate for a certain amount of time at a certain cost.

lock-in period   The time period during which the lender has guaranteed an interest rate to a borrower.

margin   The difference between the interest rate and the index on an adjustable rate mortgage. The margin remains stable over the life of the loan, while the index moves up and down.

market analysis   The study of current supply and demand conditions in a particular area for a certain type of property; it indicates marketability of properties to discern the need for and probable potential of a real estate project.

maturity   The date on which the principal balance of a loan, bond, or other financial instrument becomes due and payable.

merged credit report   A credit report that reports the raw data pulled from two or more of the major credit repositories. Contrast with a Residential Mortgage Credit Report (RMCR) or a standard factual credit report.

modification   Occasionally, a lender will agree to modify the terms of your mortgage without requiring you to refinance. If any changes are made, it is called a modification.

mortgage   A legal document that pledges a property to the lender as security for payment of a debt. Instead of mortgages, some states use First Trust Deeds.

mortgage banker   Originates and funds its own loans, which are then sold on the secondary market, usually to Fannie Mae, Freddie Mac, or Ginnie Mae.

mortgage broker   A mortgage company that originates loans, then places those loans with a variety of other lending institutions with whom they usually have pre-established relationships.

mortgagee   The lender in a mortgage agreement.

mortgage insurance (MI)   Insurance that covers the lender against some of the losses incurred as a result of a default on a home loan.

mortgage insurance premium (MIP)   The amount paid by a mortgagor for mortgage insurance, either to a government agency such as the Federal Housing Administration (FHA) or to a private mortgage insurance (MI) company.

mortgage life and disability insurance A type of term life insurance often bought by borrowers. The amount of coverage decreases as the principal balance declines. Some policies also cover the borrower in the event of disability. In the event that the borrower dies while the policy is in force, the debt is automatically satisfied by insurance proceeds. In the case of disability insurance, the insurance will make the mortgage payment for a specified amount of time during the disability.

mortgagor The borrower in a mortgage agreement.

multi dwelling units Properties that provide separate housing units for more than one family, although they secure only a single mortgage.

negative amortization Some adjustable rate mortgages allow the interest rate to fluctuate independently of a required minimum payment. If a borrower makes the minimum payment it may not cover all of the interest that would normally be due at the current interest rate. In essence, the borrower defers the interest payment, which is added to the balance of the loan. The loan balance grows larger instead of smaller, which is called negative amortization.

no cash-out refinance A refinance transaction which is not intended to put cash in the hand of the borrower. Instead, the new balance is calculated to cover the balance due on the current loan and any costs associated with obtaining the new mortgage. Often referred to as a "rate and term refinance."

note A legal document that obligates a borrower to repay a mortgage loan at a stated interest rate during a specified period of time.

note rate The interest rate stated on a mortgage note.

notice of default A formal written notice to a borrower that a default has occurred and that legal action may be taken.

original principal balance The total amount of principal owed on a mortgage before any payments are made.

origination fee On a government loan, the loan origination fee is 1 percent of the loan amount, but additional points may be charged which are called "discount points." One point equals 1 percent of the loan amount. On a conventional loan, the loan origination fee refers to the total number of points a borrower pays.

owner financing A property purchase transaction in which the property seller provides all or part of the financing.

partial payment   A payment that is not sufficient to cover the scheduled monthly payment on a mortgage loan. Normally, a lender will not accept a partial payment, but in times of hardship you can make this request of the loan servicing collection department.

payment change date   The date when a new monthly payment amount takes effect on an adjustable-rate mortgage (ARM) or a graduated-payment mortgage (GPM). Generally, the payment change date occurs in the month immediately after the interest rate adjustment date.

periodic payment cap   For an adjustable-rate mortgage where the interest rate and the minimum payment amount fluctuate independently of one another, this is a limit on the amount that payments can increase or decrease during any one adjustment period.

periodic rate cap   For an adjustable-rate mortgage, a limit on the amount that the interest rate can increase or decrease during any one adjustment period, regardless of how high or low the index might be.

personal property   Any property that is not real property.

PITI   An abbreviation for principal, interest, taxes, and insurance. If you have an "impounded" loan, then your monthly payment to the lender includes all of these and probably includes mortgage insurance as well. If you do not have an impounded account, then the lender still calculates this amount and uses it as part of determining your debt-to-income ratio.

PITI reserves   A cash amount that a borrower must have on hand after making a down payment and paying all closing costs for the purchase of a home. The principal, interest, taxes, and insurance (PITI) reserves must equal the amount that the borrower would have to pay for PITI for a predefined number of months.

planned unit development (PUD)   A type of ownership where individuals actually own the building or unit they live in, but common areas are owned jointly with the other members of the development or association. Contrast with condominium, where an individual actually owns the airspace of his unit, but the buildings and common areas are owned jointly with the others in the development or association.

point   A point is 1 percent of the amount of the mortgage.

power of attorney A legal document that authorizes another person to act on one's behalf. A power of attorney can grant complete authority or can be limited to certain acts and/or certain periods of time.

pre-approval A loosely used term which is generally taken to mean that a borrower has completed a loan application and provided debt, income, and savings documentation which an underwriter has reviewed and approved. A pre-approval is usually done for a certain loan amount and makes assumptions about what the interest rate will actually be at the time the loan is actually made. It also estimates the borrower's property taxes, insurance costs, and other costs associated with the home purchase and ownership. A pre-approval applies only to the borrower. Once a property is chosen, it must also meet the underwriting guidelines of the lender.

prepayment Any amount paid to reduce the principal balance of a loan before the due date. Payment in full on a mortgage that may result from a sale of the property, the owner's decision to pay off the loan in full, or a foreclosure. In each case, prepayment means payment occurs before the loan has been fully amortized.

prepayment penalty A fee that may be charged to a borrower who pays off a loan before it is due.

pre-qualification This usually refers to the loan officer's written opinion of the ability of a borrower to qualify for a home loan, after the loan officer has made inquiries about debt, income, and savings. The information provided to the loan officer may have been presented verbally or in the form of documentation, and the loan officer may or may not have reviewed a credit report on the borrower.

prime rate The interest rate that banks charge to their preferred customers. Changes in the prime rate are widely publicized in the news media and are used as the indexes in some adjustable rate mortgages, especially home equity lines of credit. Changes in the prime rate do not directly affect other types of mortgages, but the same factors that influence the prime rate also affect the interest rates of mortgage loans.

principal The amount borrowed or remaining unpaid. The part of the monthly payment that reduces the remaining balance of a mortgage.

principal balance The outstanding balance of principal on a mortgage. The principal balance does not include interest or any other charges. *See* remaining balance.

principal, interest, taxes, and insurance (PITI)   The four components of a monthly mortgage payment on impounded loans. Principal refers to the part of the monthly payment that reduces the remaining balance of the mortgage. Interest is the fee charged for borrowing money. Taxes and insurance refer to the amounts that are paid into an escrow account each month for property taxes and mortgage and hazard insurance.

private mortgage insurance (MI)   Mortgage insurance that is provided by a private mortgage insurance company to protect lenders against loss if a borrower defaults. Most lenders generally require MI for a loan with a loan-to-value (LTV) percentage in excess of 80 percent.

promissory note   A written promise to repay a specified amount over a specified period of time.

public auction   A meeting in an announced public location to sell property to repay a mortgage that is in default.

purchase agreement   A written contract signed by the buyer and seller stating the terms and conditions under which a property will be sold.

purchase money transaction   The acquisition of property through the payment of money or its equivalent.

qualifying ratios   Calculations that are used in determining whether a borrower can qualify for a mortgage. There are two ratios. The "top" or "front" ratio is a calculation of the borrower's monthly housing costs (principle, taxes, insurance, mortgage insurance, homeowner's association fees) as a percentage of monthly income. The "back" or "bottom" ratio includes housing costs as will as all other monthly debt.

quitclaim deed   A deed that transfers without warranty whatever interest or title a grantor may have at the time the conveyance is made.

rate lock   A commitment issued by a lender to a borrower or other mortgage originator guaranteeing a specified interest rate for a specified period of time at a specific cost.

real estate agent   A person licensed to negotiate and transact the sale of real estate.

Real Estate Settlement Procedures Act (RESPA)   A consumer protection law that requires lenders to give borrowers advance notice of closing costs.

real property   Land and appurtenances, including anything of a permanent nature such as structures, trees, minerals, and the interest, benefits, and inherent rights thereof.

realtor A real estate agent, broker, or associate who holds active membership in a local real estate board that is affiliated with the National Association of Realtors.

recorder The public official who keeps records of transactions that affect real property in the area. Sometimes known as a "Registrar of Deeds" or "County Clerk."

recording The noting in the registrar's office of the details of a properly executed legal document, such as a deed, a mortgage note, a satisfaction of mortgage, or an extension of mortgage, thereby making it a part of the public record.

refinance transaction The process of paying off one loan with the proceeds from a new loan using the same property as security.

remaining balance The amount of principal that has not yet been repaid. *See* principal balance.

remaining term The original amortization term minus the number of payments that have been applied.

rent loss insurance Insurance that protects a landlord against loss of rent or rental value due to fire or other casualty that renders the leased premises unavailable for use and as a result of which the tenant is excused from paying rent.

repayment plan An arrangement made to repay delinquent installments or advances.

replacement reserve fund A fund set aside for replacement of common property in a condominium, PUD, or cooperative project, particularly that property which has a short life expectancy, such as carpeting or furniture.

revolving debt A credit arrangement, such as a credit card, that allows a customer to borrow against a preapproved line of credit when purchasing goods and services. The borrower is billed for the amount that is actually borrowed plus any interest due.

right of first refusal A provision in an agreement that requires the owner of a property to give another party the first opportunity to purchase or lease the property before he or she offers it for sale or lease to others.

right of ingress or egress The right to enter or leave designated premises.

right of survivorship In joint tenancy, the right of survivors to acquire the interest of a deceased joint tenant.

sale-leaseback A technique in which a seller deeds property to a buyer for a consideration, and the buyer simultaneously leases the property back to the seller.

secondary market   The buying and selling of existing mortgages, usually as part of a "pool" of mortgages.

second mortgage   A mortgage that has a lien position subordinate to the first mortgage.

secured loan   A loan that is backed by collateral.

security   The property that will be pledged as collateral for a loan.

seller carry-back   An agreement in which the owner of a property provides financing, often in combination with an assumable mortgage.

servicer   An organization that collects principal and interest payments from borrowers and manages borrowers' escrow accounts. The servicer often services mortgages that have been purchased by an investor in the secondary mortgage market.

servicing   The collection of mortgage payments from borrowers and related responsibilities of a loan servicer.

short sale   A real estate sale in which the proceeds from the sale fall short of the balance owed on a loan secured by the property sold.

subdivision   A housing development created by dividing a tract of land into individual lots for sale or lease.

subordinate financing   Any mortgage or other lien that has a priority that is lower than that of the first mortgage.

subprime mortgage   A subprime mortgage is granted to borrowers whose credit history is not sufficient to get a conventional mortgage. Often these borrowers have impaired or even no credit history. These mortgages can also include interest-only loans.

survey   A drawing or map showing the precise legal boundaries of a property, the location of improvements, easements, rights of way, encroachments, and other physical features.

sweat equity   Contribution to the construction or rehabilitation of a property in the form of labor or services rather than cash.

tenancy in common   As opposed to joint tenancy, when there are two or more individuals on title to a piece of property, this type of ownership does not pass ownership to the others in the event of death.

third-party origination   A process by which a lender uses another party to completely or partially originate, process, underwrite, close, fund, or package the mortgages it plans to deliver to the secondary mortgage market.

title   A legal document proving a person's right to or ownership of a property.

title company A company that specializes in examining and insuring real estate titles.

title insurance Insurance that protects the lender (lender's policy) or the buyer (owner's policy) against loss arising from disputes over property ownership.

title search A check of the title records to ensure that the seller is the legal owner of the property and that there are no liens or other claims outstanding.

transfer of ownership Any means by which the ownership of a property changes hands. Lenders consider all of the following situations to be a transfer of ownership: the purchase of a property "subject to" the mortgage, the assumption of the mortgage debt by the property purchaser, and any exchange of possession of the property under a land sales contract or any other land trust device.

transfer tax State or local tax payable when a property's title passes from one owner to another.

treasury index An index that is used to determine interest rate changes for certain adjustable-rate mortgage (ARM) plans. It is based on the results of auctions that the U.S. Treasury holds for its Treasury bills and securities or is derived from the U.S. Treasury's daily yield curve, which is based on the closing market bid yields on actively traded Treasury securities in the over-the-counter market.

trustee A fiduciary who holds or controls property for the benefit of another.

truth-in-lending A federal law that requires lenders to fully disclose, in writing, the terms and conditions of a mortgage, including the annual percentage rate (APR) and other charges.

two-step mortgage An adjustable-rate mortgage (ARM) that has one interest rate for the first five or seven years of its term and a different interest rate for the remainder.

two- to four-family property A property that consists of a structure that provides living space (dwelling units) for two to four families, although ownership of the structure is covered by a single deed.

VA mortgage A mortgage guaranteed by the U.S. Department of Veterans Affairs.

vested Having the right to use a portion of a fund such as an individual retirement fund. For example, individuals who are

100 percent vested can withdraw all of the funds that are set aside for them in a retirement fund. However, taxes may be due on any funds that are actually withdrawn.

Veterans Administration   An agency of the federal government that guarantees residential mortgages made to eligible veterans of the military services. The guarantee protects the lender against loss and thus encourages lenders to make mortgages to veterans.

Resources

The following resources are useful to real estate professionals at all levels of their careers. Associations and membership organizations provide valuable networking and continuing educational opportunities. Some of the books listed below cover the nuts-and-bolts facts about real estate and real estate transactions, while others focus on creating a long, fruitful career. Periodicals are vital for keeping current on breaking industry news and projected trends. Specific educational institutions are excellent "one-stop" places for seminars, conferences, advanced certifications, and other career development opportunities. Finally, selected Web sites act as storehouses of information about all realms of the real estate industry.

Associations, Societies, and Membership Organizations

Affordable Housing Investors Council (AHIC) is a nonprofit organization comprising corporations engaged in the investment of funds for affordable housing. (http://www.ahic.org)

Affordable Housing Tax Credit Coalition is a group of developers, syndicators, lenders, nonprofit groups, public agencies, and others concerned with the low-income housing tax credit. (http://www.taxcreditcoalition.org)

American Association of Small Property Owners is a national organization for small landlords and real estate investors. (http://www.smallpropertyowner.com)

American Industrial Real Estate Association claims to be nation's largest and most respected organization of industrial and commercial real estate brokers. (http://www.airea.com)

American Institute of Architects (AIA) is one of the largest national organizations for architects and those interested in the field of architecture. It has approximately 80,000 members. (http://www.aia.org)

American Planning Association (APA) dedicates itself to advancing the art and science of urban, rural and regional planning. They have approximately 30,000 members. (http://www.planning.org)

American Real Estate and Urban Economics Association (AREUEA) was founded in 1964 and focuses on the need for more information and analysis in the fields of real estate development, planning, and economics. (http://www.areua.org)

Fast Facts

Joining a Trade Association

Why should you join a real estate trade association? Here is a list of some of the top reasons joining one is a great career move:

- Networking: In the real estate industry, networking is number one. At association meetings you meet potential employers as well as clients.

- Information: The industry is constantly changing. Most associations publish newsletters, journals, or magazines with the latest industry news, trends, and technologies. Many also offer seminars and conferences led by key leaders in the field.

- Advocacy: There is strength in numbers. Large associations often employ top lobbyists who advocate for new laws or revising existing laws for the betterment of the industry and represent your interests as a real estate professional.

- Jobs: Several associations offer job boards, postings, or other employment services.

American Real Estate Society (ARES) is a society of and for high-level practicing professionals and real estate professors at colleges and universities throughout the United States and the world. (http://www.aresnet.org)

American Senior Housing Association (ASHA) provides leadership for the senior housing industry on legislative and regulatory matters, and promotes research and the exchange of information among the developers, operators, and financiers of all types of senior housing. (http://www.seniorshousing.org)

American Society of Farm Managers and Rural Appraisers is an association for rural appraisal, real property review appraisal, and farm managers. (http://www.asfmra.org)

Appraisal Institute (AI) is an international membership association of professional real estate appraisers, with more than 18,000 members and 99 chapters throughout the United States, Canada, and abroad. (http://www.appraisalinstitute.org)

Association of Construction Inspectors (ACI) is an organization for those involved in construction inspection and construction project management. (http://www.aci-assoc.org)

Association of Foreign Investors in U.S. Real Estate (AFIRE) is a trade association for the foreign real estate investment community whose members have a common interest in preserving and promoting international real estate investment. (http://www.afire.com)

Association of Real Estate License Law Officials (ARELLO) comprises the official governmental agencies and other organizations around the world that issue real estate licenses/registrations in addition to regulating real estate practice and enforcing real estate law. (http://www.arello.com)

Builders Owners and Managers Association (BOMA) was founded in 1907. Today BOMA International represents 100 North American and nine overseas associations in Australia, Brazil, Finland, Indonesia, Japan, Korea, the Philippines, and South Africa. (http://www.boma.org)

Certified International Property Specialist Network (CIPSN) is a specialty group of the National Association of Realtors with over 1,500 members focusing on international real estate business. (http://www.realtor.org)

Counselors of Real Estate (CRE) is a professional membership organization for real estate advisers who have been recognized by their peers and clients for their high level knowledge, experience, and integrity. All members of the organization hold the CRE designation, which is bestowed by invitation only. (http://www.cre.org)

Electronic Financial Services Council (EFSC) is an association dedicated solely to promoting changes in law necessary to facilitate the electronic delivery of financial services. (http://www.efscouncil.org)

Environmental Assessment Association (EAA) is an international organization for those involved with environmental inspections, testing, and hazardous material removal with approximately 5,000 members. (http://www.iami.org)

Housing Inspection Foundation is an organization of professionals dedicated to the promotion and development of home inspection. (http://www.iami.org)

Institute for Luxury Homes Marketing is an association for agents who work in the upper-tier residential market around the world. (http://www.luxuryhomemarketing.com)

Institute of Property Taxation (IPT) is a nonprofit educational association serving more than 4,000 members. (http://www.ipt.org)

Institute of Real Estate Management (IREM) is an association of property and asset managers. An affiliate of the National Association of Realtors, this organization is a source for education, resources, and information for people in the real estate industry. (http://www.irem.org)

International Consortium of Real Estate Association (ICREA) is an affiliate of NAR with a global alliance whose members are leading national real estate organizations in the world's major markets. (http://www.icrea.org)

International Council of Shopping Centers (ICSC) was founded in 1957. ICSC is the global trade association of the shopping center industry with approximately 40,000 members. (http://www.icsc.org)

International Real Estate Institute (IREI) was founded in 1975 and serves international real estate members in over 100 nations. (http://www.iami.org)

International Real Estate Society (IRES) is a federation of regional real estate societies. Each Society maintains control over its own activities while participating in the federation to get the benefits of global co-operation. (http://www.iresnet.org)

Mortgage Bankers Association of America (MBAA) was founded 1914 as the Farm Mortgage Bankers Association. Today MBAA is the largest Association representing the real estate finance industry with some 2,800 members involved in real estate finance. (http://www.mbaa.org)

National Association of Auctioneers (NAA) promotes the auction method of marketing and enhances the professionalism of its practitioners. (http://www.auctioneers.org)

National Association of Development Organizations (NADO) provides training, information and representation for regional development organizations in small metropolitan and rural America. (http://www.nado.org)

National Association of Exclusive Buyer's Agents (NAEBA) was founded in 1995 to enhance and promote buyer representation skills and services. (http://www.naeba.com)

National Association of Home Builders (NAHB) is a federation of more than 800 state and local builders associations. About one-third of NAHB's more than 200,00 members are homebuilders and/or remodelers. (http://www.nahb.com)

National Association of Independent Fee Appraisers (NAIFA) is all about being in a professional family of appraisers from its candidate members up through the ranks to our national officers. (http://www.naifa.com)

National Association of Industrial and Office Properties (NAIOP) is a national association with over 9,500 members and network of 47 chapters that represent the interests of developers and owners of industrial, office, and related commercial real estate. (http://www.naiop.org)

National Association of Master Appraisers (NAMA) was founded in 1982 and dedicated to promoting professionalism in the real estate appraisal industry. (http://www.masterappraisers.org)

National Association of Mortgage Brokers (NAMB) is an association dedicated to the improvement of the mortgage brokerage industry. (http://www.namb.org)

National Association of Professional Mortgage Women (NAPMW) is the premier network of individuals within the mortgage community that promotes professional and personal development for women through educational and leadership opportunities. (http://www.napmw.org)

National Association of Real Estate Appraisers (NAREA) was founded in 1966 to make available highly qualified real estate

Keeping
in Touch

Networking

Let's face it, not everyone is into doing the networking thing. Despite the fact that most real estate professionals are salespeople, networking can still be a hard thing for many to do. Practicing and delivering a canned introduction while working the crowd can feel forced, phony, and like a lot of work. Experts today advocate losing the old mindset of simply looking for people who can help your career. Instead, identify people you are genuinely interested in getting to know. Also remember to give as much as you receive. When you genuinely want to help others, they are more likely to return the favor. Here are a few things you can gain from this kind of approach to networking:

- At the least, new friendships with those you may not have met elsewhere.
- Relationships with others interested in the real estate industry who can give you a new perspective.
- Connections with other real estate agents, brokers, and companies.
- First knowledge of jobs and promotions at other companies.
- Pass it forward opportunities—if they cannot help you, they may know someone who can.

appraisers to those requiring professional appraisal reports. (http://www.iami.org)

National Association of Real Estate Consultants (NAREC) was founded in 1999 to assist real estate professionals in reframing their focus as real estate consultants to better meet the needs of today's savvy consumer. (http://www.narec.com)

National Association of Real Estate Investment Trusts (NAREIT) is an association for real estate companies that are real estate investment trusts (REITs) and other businesses that own, operate, and finance income-producing real estate. (http://www.nareit.com)

National Association of Realtors (NAR) is the "voice of real estate." With 1,400,000 members is America's largest professional association. (http://www.realtor.org)

National Association of Residential Property Managers (NARPM) is an association of real estate professionals who know first-hand the unique problems and challenges of managing single-family and small residential properties. (http://www.narpm.org)

National Housing Conference (NHC) is an association dedicated to advancing affordable housing and community development causes. (http://www.nhc.org)

National Leased Housing Association (NLHA) represents all major participants, both private and public, in the multifamily rental housing industry. (http://www.hudnlha.com)

National Multi Housing Council (NMHC) is an association representing the interests of the nation's larger and most prominent apartment firms. (http://www.nmhc.org)

Real Estate Buyers Agent Council (REBAC) was founded in 1988 to promote buyer representation skills and services. It has been an affiliate of the National Association of Realtors since 1996. (http://www.rebac.net)

Real Estate Information Professional Association (REIPA) is an association for professionals and corporations involved in providing real estate and public record information in the United States. (http://www.reipa.org)

Real Estate Investment Advisory Council (REIAC) is an association that provides an open forum for the exchange of ideas, concerns and experiences between people who conduct commercial real estate transactions. (http://www.reiac.org)

Real Estate Professionals Society (REPS) is dedicated to increasing professionalism of agents across the entire real estate spectrum including residential and commercial real estate, mortgage, appraisal and home inspection. (http://www.realestateprofessionalssociety.com)

Realtors Land Institute (RLI) is an affiliate of the National Association of Realtors that focuses on land brokerage transactions of five specialized types: farms and ranches, undeveloped tracts of land, transitional and development land, subdivision and wholesaling of lots, and site selection and assemblage of land parcels. (http://www.rliland.com)

Senior Advantage Real Estate Council (SAREC) is an association that assists realtors in meeting the special real estate needs and concerns of maturing Americans. (http://www.seniorsrealestate .com)

Women's Council of Realtors (WCR) is a community of real estate professionals creating business opportunities, for females in the real estate brokerage industry. (http://www.wcr.org)

Books and Periodicals

Books

Barron's Real Estate Handbook, **3rd ed.** By Jack C. Harris (Barron's Educational Series, 1993). With a glossary of more than 2,000 real estate terms and expressions, as well as sample legal documents and financial forms, this book serves as a fine survey for established professionals and novice agents alike. Special focus is given to architectural styles and trends as well as zoning laws, while numerous illustrations, charts, and graphs help clarify more intricate concepts.

Branding The Real Estate Agent. By Mark Hughes and Amy Young (BookSurge Publishing, 2008). Coauthored by one of the top 1 percent of real estate agents in the world, this book is geared towards those who wish to build their own real estate business. It features tips on how to develop and burnish one's reputation, improve client relations, and add a personal touch to routine sales transactions.

How to Become a Power Agent in Real Estate: A Top Industry Trainer Explains How to Double Your Income in 12 Months. By Darryl Davis (McGraw-Hill, 2002). Based on the author's very popular seminar "The Power Program," this book details the best ways to improve real estate sales. Areas covered include: surefire ways to find prospective sellers, how to effectively dialogue with reluctant buyers, the best tactics for self-promotion, agent-tested methods of time management, and many more.

How to Prepare for the Real Estate Licensing Exams: Salesperson, Broker, Appraiser, **7th ed.** By Jack P. Friedman (Barron's Educational Series, 2005). This comprehensive study guide features nine full-length practice exams that will prepare students for licensing tests in all 50 states. With more than 1,500 practice questions and answers as well as a complete glossary of real estate terms and expressions, it is an excellent primer for anyone serious about attaining certification.

The Millionaire Real Estate Agent: It's Not About the Money . . . It's About Being the Best You Can Be! By Gary Keller, Dave Jenks, and Jay Papasan (McGraw-Hill, 2004). This book examines different financial models and ways to increase earning power, though is careful to differentiate between the pursuit of excellence and that of crass materialism. It offers a more holistic, personal approach to developing one's total self within the framework of a real estate career.

Modern Real Estate Practice, **14th ed.** By Fillmore W. Galaty, Wellington J. Allaway, and Robert C. Kyle (Dearborn Financial Publishing, 1996). This book is an ideal study guide for those preparing for their real estate license certification exams. The new edition covers such cutting-edge topics as the role of the intermediary agent, the impact of environmental regulations on the industry, and the rise of Internet-based sales.

Online Marketing Techniques for Real Estate Agents and Brokers. By Karen Vieira (Atlantic Publishing Co., 2008). This book focuses on the groundbreaking trend of Internet sales as a tool for real estate agents. Learn the basics of online advertising, electronic mailing lists, building Web communities, and other skills necessary to interface with your clientele in the digital age.

Opportunities in Real Estate Careers. By Mariwyn Evans (VGM Career Horizons, 1997). Written by a seasoned veteran of the real estate industry who has developed many instructional methods used to train new agents, this book covers all essential information needed for anyone thinking about a career in real estate.

Perfect Phrases for Real Estate Agents & Brokers. By Dan Hamilton (CWL Publishing Enterprises, 2009). Something of a comprehensive industry glossary, this book compiles the many industry terms, expressions, and phrases that can give salespeople an added lift in closing a deal. In an industry where verbal communication is key to making things happen, the dialogues outlined in this book (as well as descriptions of hypothetical situations commonly encountered by agents) will prove essential to continued success.

The Real Book of Real Estate: Real Experts. Real Stories. Real Life. By Robert T. Kiyosaki (Vanguard Press, 2009). Drawing on the expert advice of the author's closest associates, this book features key insights into the industry and the secrets of finding hidden development opportunities.

Real Estate Careers: 25 Growing Opportunities. By Carolyn Janik and Ruth Rejnis (John Wiley & Sons, 1994). Divided into features on 25 different real estate careers, this guide is ideal for someone who wishes to explore his or her potential place within the industry. It helps assess the reader's strengths and tailors them to an appropriate career.

SHIFT: How Top Real Estate Agents Tackle Tough Times. By Gary Keller (McGraw-Hill, 2010). Especially appropriate in moments of industry transition, this New York Times bestseller delves into the best methods for achieving success in any market. It focuses on such topics as tapping into the foreclosure market and dealing with hesitant buyers.

Your First Year in Real Estate: Making the Transition from Total Novice to Successful Professional. By Dirk Zeller (Three Rivers Press, 2001). Taking a step-by-step approach to the development of a long-term real estate career, this book offers all the practical advice you need to get off to a great start in the industry. Learn how to find mentors, gain a solid client base, and set and prioritize essential career goals.

Your Successful Real Estate Career, **5th ed.** By Kenneth W. Edwards (AMACOM Books, 2006). One of the bestselling real estate books of all time, this is the ideal introductory volume for the novice agent. It gives a thorough overview of the industry, as well as descriptions of challenges (and opportunities) new agents typically encounter. Long cited by industry professionals, the new edition features a special focus on current technology and how it is changing the practice of buying and selling real estate.

Periodicals

Journal of Property Management, the official publication of the Institute of Real Estate Management in Chicago, Illinois, is specifically tailored to asset and property managers of U.S. investment real estate. (http://www.irem.org)

Personal Real Estate Investor Magazine is full of tips for the novice and the experienced investor alike. (http://www.personalrealestateinvestormag.com)

Real Estate Magazine is the official publication of RISMedia. Its focus is primarily on real estate information systems and the uses

Problem
Solving

Keeping up with Real Estate Industry
News and Trends

Professionals in the real estate industry practically work
around the clock as it is. Who has time to read? But staying
informed of the latest trends and news is critical for building success. Here are some timesaving ways to stay on top of the informa-
tional curve:

- E-newsletters: E-newsletters from real estate trade associations
  are usually free and open to anyone—you do not have to be a
  member. Each day as you check your e-mail you can also take a
  few minutes to scan the latest news.

- Podcasts: Podcasts are downloadable audio bites. You can down-
  load them to your computer or MP3 player and listen to them at
  your convenience, when you are on the road, or shuffling through
  paperwork at the office. There are many podcasts available in the
  real estate industry through associations and businesses.

- RSS feeds: There are real estate news feeds Web sites like realty-
  feedsearch.com that offers those in the industry a place to get the
  latest news. Subscribers can also post the RSS feeds to their own
  Web sites.

of online social networking and Web-based applications for real
estate sales. (http://livemag.rismedia.com)

Real Estate Portfolio is a well-respected industry periodical that reg-
ularly features interviews with industry leaders. It also provides
a national focus by following specific pieces of national legislation
and their effects on the real estate market. (http://www.nareit
.com/portfoliomag/default.shtml)

Realtor Magazine is one of the most comprehensive periodicals for
real estate professionals today. It delves into industry trends, ethical issues facing realtors, the impact of technology on the workplace, and many other topics. Web-based seminars and e-mail
newsletters are key features for subscribers. (http://www.realtor
.org/rmohome/home)

Web Sites

The Appraisal Foundation is a nonprofit organization devoted to advancing best practices and universal standards of appraising. It works to establish licensing criteria as well as sponsor gatherings and networking opportunities for appraisers. Its Web site is an excellent portal to the many services it offers. (http://www.appraisalfoundation.org)

FindLaw's State-Specific Real Estate Forms is a Web-based archive of real estate forms, including deeds, liens, contracts, and other standard legal procedures for various states. (http://www.uslegalforms.com/findlaw/realestate)

National Association of Realtors' Code of Ethics is a complete listing of official ethical bylaws as agreed upon by the NAR. (http://www.realtor.org/mempolweb.nsf/pages/code)

"The 1929 Stock Market Crash" is an excellent overview of the causes and legacy of the infamous catastrophic event. (http://eh.net/encyclopedia/article/Bierman.Crash)

Real Estate and Mortgage Resources is an excellent clearinghouse for articles and information on buying and selling property. It enables the user to find realtors, calculate the value of a home, and search property listings, among other things. (http://www.realestateabc.com)

The Real Estate Professional is an online magazine for industry professionals, featuring industry news, articles on current trends, and reviews of publications by internationally respected authors. (http://www.therealestatepro.com)

Education

Florida State University Center for Real Estate Education and Research is known for facilitating extensive networking between students, alumni, and professional friends of the university. Yearly events include conferences, speaking engagements, and roundtable discussions on current trends in the real estate industry. (http://www.fsurealestate.com)

Green Real Estate Education prides itself on conducting the only course in the United States on "green" building. Emphasis is placed on developing energy efficient homes, and is applicable to all real estate professions—from appraisers and inspectors to handymen and electricians. (http://greenrealestateeducation.com/green)

Ivy Real Estate School of Education is a training facility run by real estate guidance counselors licensed by the state of New York. The organization features a monthly job fair that helps graduates connect with brokers and other industry professionals. (http://www.nyrealed.com)

Real Estate Express is the nation's oldest online real estate license school. It has consistently proven itself ahead of the game as more and more people pursue their license training courses through the Internet. The program covers exam preparation for most states, as well as pre-license, post-license, broker, and continuing education courses. It has successfully trained over 100,000 real estate students from all across the nation. (http://www.realestateexpress.com)

Realty U offers brokers and agents a diverse array of career development services, with special focus on honing executive and leadership skills. It utilizes both traditional classroom and Internet-based teaching applications. (http://www.realtyu.com)

Index